LETTING GO DOWN BELOW:

7 Steps to Freedom of Expulsion

Unleash your inner windhorse and shed the shackles of pseudo-civilization!

Interactive Rip-While-U-Read™ Edition

First Published in Great Britain 2019 by Mirador Publishing
Second edition published in Norway 2024 by the author under imprint Breakwind Pubs

Copyright © 2019, 2024 by Chris Darewind

All rights reserved. No part of this publication may be reproduced or transmitted, in any form or by any means, without permission of the author. Excepting brief quotes used in reviews.

First edition: 2019
Second edition: 2024

Any reference to real names and places are purely fictional and are constructs of the author. Any offense the references produce is unintentional and in no way reflects the reality of any locations or people involved.

A copy of this work is available through the Norwegian National Library.

ISBN: 978-82-693834-0-9

Breakwind Pubs
c/o Inge Christian Rakvaag
Valhallveien 9
N-0196 Oslo
Norway

LETTING GO DOWN BELOW:

7 Steps to Freedom of Expulsion

By CHRIS DAREWIND

Contents

Introduction	7
1. Everybody Knows That Everybody Farts, Including the Emperor	11
2. Essential Ideas and Concepts	21
3. How to Bring the Ideas in This Book to Life	30
4. Step 1: Acknowledge That We Are Human Beings and Prepare to Subvert Against the Robots	48
5. Step 2: Fart Because It's Good for You	55
6. Step 3: Look to Man's Best Friend	65
7. Step 4: Fart Around the Guys/Girls	72
8. Step 5: Fart in the Presence of Your Partner	77
9. Step 6: Fart in the Presence of Authority	84
10. Step 7: Look People in the Eyes When You Fart—And Enjoy It!	100
11. Conclusion	109
Appendix: Process for Determining Social Acceptability of Biologically Driven Human Behavior	117
Acknowledgements	120

Introduction

Gargoyle "Free Farter" on the internet and you get a measly 240 hits, such as discussion forum posts. Some of the hits aren't actually about Free Farters but about apps you can buy for your cellular phone. Do the same thing with "Freemason", and you get millions of hits. Yet we all know that there are far more plain free people in the world than there are Freemasons. And we all know that we all fart, so I can guarantee you that Free Farters outnumber Freemasons by hundreds of millions to one.

Then why the low number of web pages containing "Free Farter"?

Since most people who will read this book are free—or at least live in a free country—the only plausible explanation is that people hesitate to acknowledge that they are farters in the first place. These people are in denial. Denial is bad. Start denying who you are, and Ibsenesque life lies start piling up. If you want to panic and Edit-Undo your entire life on your deathbed, denial is the way to go.

This book is about accepting who we are and how to live our lives as we were created: as eaters, kissers, dreamers, sneezers, ear wax producers, farters and many other creatures in one. We as humans think we are civilized just because we wear clothing, cook food and frown upon farting. To me, this is not civilization, it's pseudo-civilization. The shackles of pseudo-civilization weigh heavy on us. It's time we shed them and live as free, intelligent animals. Becoming a Free Farter is a major step in the right direction.

The term "Free Farter" is also a double entendre: farting freely is a goal in itself, but becoming free-spirited is the ultimate goal. As we are all farters, you automatically become a Free Farter once you liberate yourself and find inner peace—literally.

The best way to achieve this inner peace is to search for your inner windhorse and unleash it upon your environment, the system people tend to call civilization. We all know it's just an empty shell. This book tells you how to break free.

Eight Key Ideas Developed Throughout This Book

Key Idea # 1: *Believing that celebrities and politicians don't fart is a threat to democracy*

Key Idea # 2: *With robots taking over nearly every aspect of human life—and eventually the entire planet—***farting may be our only hope if we are to survive as a species***

Key Idea # 3: *People who deliberately fart alone are selfish*

Key Idea # 4: *Farting may help you financially*

Key Idea # 5: *If in doubt whether you should fart, ask yourself, "Would a dog fart here?"*

Key Idea # 6: *Farting can help you find a suitable partner to procreate with*

Key Idea # 7: *Freedom is natural, never forced*

Key Idea # 8: *People who tell you to stop farting are evil*

1.
Everybody Knows That Everybody Farts, Including the Emperor

"I am, therefore I fart." — Desfartes

Algiers, '42

" I waited. The heat was beginning to burn my face; small drops of sweat were starting to gather in my eyebrows. It was just as disagreeably hot as at my mother's funeral, and the veins in my forehead seemed to be bursting through my skin. I couldn't stand it any longer, so I took another step forward without actually moving out of the sun. And then the Rabid One inhaled smoke from his cigar and opened his mouth to let the smoke plume's menacing tentacles find their way to my face, blocking the sunlight. A dense, narrow smoke plume shot upward from the cigar, and I felt as if a long, thin blade pierced through my forehead. Then the sweat in my eyebrows poured down on my eyelids, covering them with a moist, warm film that nearly blinded me; I was conscious only of the cymbals of the sun banging on my head, and, less distinctly, of the sharp-smelling smoke emanating from the cigar, scratching my cornea, and poking into my eyeballs. Then everything began to reel before my eyes, an unbearably hot gust came from the sea, while the sky split in two in a loud crack, from end to end, and a great sheet of flame poured down through the rift. Every nerve in my body was a steel spring, and my buttocks' grip failed to retain the flammable gas inside me. My sphincter dilated in a swift, oscillating movement barely visible to the naked eye—had one been in a position to observe —and the compressed yet smooth, warm whiff briefly caressed my soft perianal skin. And so, with that spine-shaking, trumpet-like sound, it all began. I shook off my sweat and the clinging veil of light. I realized I'd crushed the equilibrium of the day, the spacious calm of this beach from which I had happy memories. But I let four more farts fly into his awestruck face, on which they obviously left no visible trace. And each successive fart was another loud, fateful rap on the door of my descent into annihilation. I was questioned several times immediately after the citizens' arrest. But they were all formal interrogations, as to my name and address and so forth. At the first of these, which took place at the lifeguards' office, nobody seemed to have much interest in the case. Then they inquired if I had anything to say in my defense. I answered, 'No,' I hadn't thought about it, and asked him if it was necessary for me to justify my behavior.

'Why do you ask that?' he said. I replied that I considered my case as very straightforward. He smiled. 'Well, that's what you think.' When leaving, I was about to shake his hand and say, 'Goodbye'; then I quickly remembered that I'd farted in a man's face."

Dramatic as this account may sound, we have all been there. We have all felt the natural urge to fart in an awkward moment and given in, and felt the piercingly critical stares from hypocrites witnessing our behavior.

Dublin, May 2002

A similar, although not quite as intimidating incident, took place in Dublin after the turn of the century. Here's the story, told by a Norwegian who chooses to remain anonymous for fear of retaliation by those affected.

"Joyful chatter was slowly but surely transforming into light clamor filled with a blend of suspicion and contempt. Imaginary pitchforks were shooting up like mushrooms across the drinking establishment. Instinctively but foolishly, the crowd kept their equally imaginary torches unlit for fear of a gas explosion. A man was observed tearing up a pillow, and another was filling a bucket with a low-viscosity tar that the local producer claims is good for toucans.

'What kind of people would do this?'

The woman uttering those words, an attractive American in her late twenties, spoke with a trembling voice fraught with despair and resignation over the hopeless situation she and her mates were in: trapped in a bar in a foreign country, infiltrated by an insidious enemy wreaking havoc beyond anyone's imagination.

As a build-up to these perceived atrocities, we—the Viking invaders of the New Millennium—had spent several days filling up on ample quantities of flatus-inducing liquids containing water, hops, barley and yeast. Our aim was to accumulate the firing power required to unleash a broadside of hitherto unsmelled potency, at least to that day in the history of Dublin's fair city. Possibly even our forerunners of a long-gone era would have returned aghast to their longships, had they been met by a resistance armed to their anuses with biological weapons capable of neutralizing scores of enemy troops in a single salvo.

What stirred the crowd's ill feeling was not solely the unpleasant smell. There were more important things at stake. Nearly all social energy and romantic spark were irretrievably lost for the evening. The value of universally funny jokes, carefully timed compliments and seemingly casual touches was close to zero. To add insult to injury, the guests were facing the need to dry clean all garments they were wearing, professionally clean jewelry and watches, and get a hold of the best deep cleanse skin and hair products money can buy. We're easily talking a total bill of 100 dollars or more.

We simply had to get out of there for fear of ending up paying for all that dry cleaning, or worse—rolled in that gooey drink and feathers."

The irony of a witch hunt for rogue farters taking place in a country where farting was a performing art in the 16th century, is just mind-boggling. Although they probably didn't know, the Viking invaders simply emulated the *braigetoír* depicted in *The Image of Irelande* by John Derrick, with bards and harpers trying in vain to outshine the two professional farters. Sadly, some people don't know their limits and are destined to public humiliation.

I am sure you have been in similar situations many times, where the urge to fart was uncontrollable or influenced by external factors. Maybe it wasn't quite as dramatic as what the Strange Farter experienced on the beach in North Africa, ending in tough questioning by the anti-farting vigilantes and being permanently banned from public beaches. A more important question is: how did you feel when you farted audibly in the presence of other people?

Did you feel like you were behaving naturally? Free? Or ill-behaved?

Don't Fart in Uncle Christian's Face!

I once farted in my four-year-old nephew's face, while walking up the stairs at his parents' wedding. I was wearing a Christian The Odor tuxedo, so it probably appeared an odd and out-of-place thing to do. But even if we dress to the occasion—including weddings, Nobel Prize ceremonies or graduation day, we can't eliminate or suppress basic biological needs, at least not for long. A friend of mine once commented at a National Day celebration in Norway, where people tend to wear their absolute Sunday best, "Do these people defecate?", suggesting that they looked too perfect with their national costumes and shiny silver ornaments and white blouses without so much as a speck of near-invisible dust. There simply had to be another way for the blonde demigoddesses with their subtle charm drawing attention from locals and visitors alike. Is there a pill, some sort of surgical removal of biological waste, or are these beings so perfect that there simply is zero waste production? Well, I have news for you: these near-perfect beings produce and dispose of the exact same fluids, semi-solids and gases as the rest of us. And that's exactly what I did at my sister's wedding, with the risk of being looked at with a queer look or even asked to leave the premises. As it happens, my nephew was the only witness to the event. What goes around, comes around, they say. Less than half an hour later, the tables were turned. My nephew walked up the same stairs, with me behind him. With my face only twelve to eighteen inches or so away from his butt, a loud fart was heard all the way down to the bottom of the stairs, where his mother—my sister—witnessed the youngster's transgression in utter disbelief, partly due to the occasion, partly due to the act itself.

- "Kenneth, you can't fart in Uncle Christian's face!"

- "But he farted in my face!"

- "Of course he didn't! You should not even say that."

- "But he did too!"

- "Stop saying that. You heard me, young man!"

Silence. Silence from Kenneth, and from me. I did not defend him, nor did I reprimand him. How could I? Not only did he have a genuine biological need, and not only did he idolize me—I had done the exact same thing only minutes earlier.

At the time, I did not espouse my current view that a free man or woman should do as he pleases, as long as there is no harm done to others, and any discomfort is negligible and transient. What can I say? I was young and stupid, I guess.

Everybody Knows That Everybody Farts

Millions of pages have been written about the history of human civilization. There are various theories about our origin, how and when Europe was populated by humans, the reasons for the fall of the Mayan empire, the origin of the Basque language, and so forth. Some people claim we didn't actually make it to the Moon and that the whole thing was staged by NASA, aided by Bollywood. Scientists may agree, disagree, launch a spin-off theory, or ridicule one another. And they do. But no research or academic debate is needed for this hypothesis: if there is one single statement about humanity that qualifies as an eternal truth, it's the fact that everybody knows that everybody farts. Most—

perhaps even all—generalizations about human behavior are at best open to debate, and in many cases downright falsehoods or Western propaganda. We call humans the most advanced species on Earth, we think that all parents love their children, and we believe that the world is becoming a better place to live due to technological advances and peace talks. Yet we only need to pick up a newspaper or scroll past the fake news on a news website to realize that none of this is true.

A single indisputable fact remains: **everybody knows that everybody farts**. I am not a scientist by training, but I know a foregone conclusion when I smell one.

Nobody secretly wonders if you have done it, how often you do it, how old you were the first time, whether you prefer doing it in the shower or on the couch, or which variants you indulge in. We all know that you fart, your mother farts, and the Pope farts. Period. End of debate, if ever there was one.

Fathers don't worry that daughters date farters or ask why they are wearing a short skirt when going to a school dance. "Are you wearing that so you can easily sneak out with a boy and fart without inhibitions? I don't think so—you are staying home, young lady!" All fathers know that their daughters fart, and the boys they date fart, too.

Yet, even if we all know we fart, we all pretend only bad-mannered villains do. Fart at a bar, and everybody will point and talk behind your back the rest of the evening, as if you are a criminal or a perverted delinquent. Can you think of a more blatant example of double standards?

In the classical fairy-tale, *The Emperor's New Underwear*, by

Hans Christian Undressin, the little boy wouldn't have yelled "The Emperor's underwear is soiled" or "The Emperor just farted", because we pretend nobody farts, especially royalty, clergy and celebrities. Why do we elevate such people to demigods, when in fact they are made of flesh and blood like the rest of us? We are doing ourselves a disservice by believing that they are superhumans who never need to fart. It creates an artificial distance between us and them, which makes them more susceptible to corruption, abuse of power, and clinging on to power for longer than they deserve, often through foul play.

Believing that celebrities and politicians don't fart is a threat to democracy
(Key Idea # 1)

We should demand that anyone running for office make a public statement about their farting frequency, ideally corroborated by impartial observers. If anyone claims he doesn't fart, we can conclude with absolute certainty that he wishes to establish or maintain an artificial distance between us and them and exploit the system, meaning you and me as taxpayers.

Imagine the credibility Her Majesty Queen Elizabeth II would have gained had she farted during her famous speech in which she characterized the year that had just passed as an "annus horribilis for me and my family" (no pun intended—I swear!). She wouldn't have had to fart loudly, just lifted one buttock discreetly, preferably more than once, and people would have had no doubt that she and her family are like the rest of us at the end of the day, with basic physical and emotional needs, everyday problems, relationship issues, and bodily functions that cannot be controlled at all times.

This book is about de-demonizing farting and farters and demonizing the anti-farting vigilantes; it's about behaving as we were created; it's about going with the flow; it's about being yourself; it's about letting go (yes, literally too). But most of all, it's about living in hope rather than fear.

By following the Seven Steps described in this book, YOUR LIFE can be built on HOPE rather than fear, and your SPIRIT will be FREE, free as the windhorse—that mythical central Asian creature that represents the energy on which the mind rides. When you have read this book and actively followed the Seven Steps, not only will you be able to consider yourself a Free Farter —you will also be mindful of how body and soul work in tandem for a Better You.

A Note on Vocabulary

I will consistently use the term "fart" throughout this book, except in quotes. The use of euphemisms to describe bodily functions signals distance, repulsion and even denial. There is nothing repulsive about farting. OK, every now and then we all have farts that smell like rotten eggs and then some, but that's beside the point. I am not going to use any of the following terms and expressions:

"**Break wind**." Windbreakers break wind; humans fart.

"**Expel gas**." Too medical. It's like using "generate intelligible sound waves" for "speak".

"**Pass gas**." Sounds like something you would hear at a molecular kitchen dinner party. "Can you pass me the gas, please? No, not that one—that's the formic acid. The other one.

Yes, that one. Thanks."

"**Cut the cheese**." What's the idea? I mean, seriously?

"**Flatulate**." Apart from being too medical, it sounds like a British last-minute apartment rental service. "Coming to campus and have nowhere to crash? Don't despair. Call 1-800-FLAT-U-L8 now!"

"**Air biscuit**." Sounds like something a mean prison guard would serve a starving prisoner-of-war. "Here, have an air biscuit. Too dry? Let me cut some cheese for you. Not happy with the service, are we? Hold the tips when you leave, then!"

"**Cut one**." Cut what? Be specific! And is anything actually being cut when we fart? I hope not.

"**Silent but deadly**." There is nothing deadly about farting. On the contrary, it proves you are alive and is good for you and—surprisingly—those around you.

As a side note, why does the expression "old fart" even exist? A fart is always newly made, although not necessarily fresh. This is bigotry at its saddest. In fact, farts are more like teenagers: they don't obey you and embarrass you in public, making you look for excuses to justify their behavior. As this book will tell you, there is nothing to excuse—farts and teenagers behave as designed by nature.

2.
Essential Ideas and Concepts

Statements You Make by Farting Freely

I am human

As a living organism, I have certain biological processes that I execute continuously or intermittently. Many of them cannot be controlled easily, and are even unavoidable altogether. Farting is one such process that makes me human, along with breathing and metabolism. Many mammals—possibly even all—fart, and I am no exception. Live with it.

I am alive

It's simple. Dead people don't fart anywhere near as often as the living. To make sure you don't get mistaken for a corpse just because you are not doing anything, fart as much as possible. In this evil world, there are delinquents who do all sorts of unspeakable things to defenseless people.

Imagine you are lying on the beach without moving for an hour and two young punks start debating whether you are dead or alive. Bets are up, and they need to settle the score. "OK, so how do we know if he's dead?". "Uhm, let me think. We can twist his big toe until the nail faces downwards or shove this straw up his nose." "Good idea! I go for the straw, I don't wanna touch a dead guy." As the second punk approaches, you accidentally fart (being alive, that's what you do), and he goes back to his accomplice, who says, "He farted, so what? Dead people do that. Go back and give it to him." You fart again, and they realize you are alive and settle the bet without subjecting you to any kind of trial or excruciating experiment.

I am free

Within the confines of the law, I do what I want. Period. Fair enough, I use my social skills to judge what is appropriate in any given situation, simply because I expect the same from other people. Should they decide to transgress, I will be the first to accept at least minor, harmless transgressions because I expect free people to behave freely. I will also be free to forgive them. And let's be clear: I do not consider farting a transgression of social etiquette. Chronic or acute constipation, however, is.

I don't pretend or put up a front

You'll never see me squeeze my buttocks together, cough on purpose when I fart or conceal my real self in any other way. I am me—nothing more, nothing less. Oh, and the fart is part of me until I decide it's not.

I am not better than you

We all breathe and fart the same air, and we have the same bodily functions as everyone else. We all sneeze, have erections in awkward situations, and fart. Just because you are able to control one of them, it doesn't make you a superhuman, so just let go. Literally. Now. Wherever you are.

I am one of the guys/girls

You can count on me accepting whatever you see as critical in life, and I expect the same from you. We all behave in a natural yet socially acceptable way, and we don't walk around thinking we are old-fashioned royalty. Modern royalty will read this book and get inspired, or be influenced by other readers who are proponents of free, natural behavior. As such, they too should aspire to become one of the guys/girls and break out from their fart-free, velvet-lined cocoons.

I want all people to be free

Apart from gross negligence and criminal acts, including corruption and embezzlement, we should be free to do whatever we please. This includes smoking cigars in white buildings or voting for populist jesters. We are born free and only need a handful of rules to govern our behavior. A rule against basic human behavior is just wrong and can never be respected. Try to ban sneezing and see what happens. Or kissing in public in a Western country. Or binge drinking in Scandinavia. People won't care.

I eat what I want

As a free human being, I eat what I want, including rotten eggs, fermented cabbage, maggots stuffed with haggis, and chick peas. Not that I am particularly fond of any of the foods mentioned, but I won't have the anti-flatulence police tell me what I should eat. If they try to stop me from farting, I will fart on them. And they should thank me (cf. *Step 2: Fart because it is good for you*).

I am approachable

This probably sounds like an oxymoron, but farting does make me more approachable. Why? Because you can approach me without fear of being shunned or ridiculed, should you happen to fart. Sneeze into your handkerchief or your elbow, but fart freely. I don't expect people to carry a fart-absorbing cloth, simply because I don't myself. Apparently, such cloths exist, and I have blacklisted the inventor forever. Not sure from what, but I have blacklisted her.

I am honest

I will never blame it on the dog. OK, if my fart smells like dog feces, I may consider it in a weak moment. Friendship means a lot to me, and I will never jeopardize any friendship, close or superficial, by telling lies to get away with what some see as rogue behavior, or for any other reason. The truth emanates from two of my orifices, at least. You should pay attention to both. Sometimes it is not pleasant, but hey! Live with it. Of course, I'll see if I can find a better toothpaste against bad breath and maybe start brushing my tongue again.

Another obvious characteristic of farts is that they are cries for help—from your anus, to be specific. Why is that? Wouldn't you cry for help if you were trapped inside dirty underwear for the bulk of your adult life, only seeing daylight outside the shower a handful of times a year? Most of us would panic after less than three seconds! "Hang on!" you say. "Naked people fart too!" Of course they do. But listen closely next time you accidentally walk by a nude beach. The fart tones are different, aren't they?

They sound lighter, more cheerful, compared with the typical sitting-on-the-couch fart. Those anuses have given up. Anuses in open air enjoy life and aren't shy about it. Much to the envy of anuses trapped in dirty underwear, they shout it out, loud and proud.

The PIPE Principle: Physical Integrity Principle of Extension

Most of you who read this book live in a free country. We can travel inside the country and most of us can travel freely to nearly 200 countries. We routinely go jogging or walk our dogs in parks. We go fishing or simply go for a stroll down the Main Street, U.S.A., or Avenida de Santa Fé in Buenos Aires for no reason other than to have a coffee or a beer, or just to go people watching. We cherish that freedom, even if we take it for granted a little too often.

What we hardly ever think about is that our bodies at any given point in time also contain waste like half-digested food and liquids, urine, stool, and—you guessed it—gases. Not only do we contain intestinal gases, but some people's bad breath qualifies as a gas or at least some sort of biological weapon. People who are about to vomit, contain vomit. Then there's snot, ear wax and a few other substances that most people tend to find repulsive, at least other people's.

The question is: do you ever hold it against people that they harbor these substances? Have you ever heard anyone—such as a bouncer—say, "I'll let you in a little later, but you need to lose the gases inside you first. I know you haven't farted, but the owner simply won't have hundreds of gallons of smelly gas inside the club. That goes for your friend, too. Inside a body or outside, I don't care. Lose it and come back. And don't forget the four pounds of gut bacteria while you're at it. It's disgusting!" It hasn't happened yet, at least not to me. Fair enough, people claim I'm full of it, but that's a different story. Anyway, maybe it was the original idea behind disembowelment? They captured prisoners-of-war, intruders and other enemies and thought, "There's no way I am going to keep that smelly bastard from the tribe across the river AND the stinky stuff and gases inside him on OUR territory. Where's the knife?"

Basically, wherever I go, I am fart, stool, urine, snot, you name it. It's part of me, it's who I am. If you invite me to a party, you also invite fart. And stool. And snot. And so on. Does anyone state their age as "X years, except my bowel contents, which is six hours old, including the stool in my colon, which is probably closer to ten"? And does anyone in his or her right mind expect guests to clean their colons before showing up at their wedding ceremony or their birthday party? Probably not, although eccentric, rich people among the readers of this book may get silly ideas. (I accept royalties in bitcoins, just for the record.) Essentially, all of me—including repelling substances—forms by definition an integral part and is as free as the physical person I represent. This means that the gas inside me is free. And the stool and the other physical matters inside me.

We are now defining the Physical Integrity Principle of Extension —PIPE—and applying it:

If and when a free person contains various naturally produced matters inside him or her, then any and all such matters are equally free, as they form an integral part of the free person's body.

The logic is that bystanders and society as a whole cannot and will not care—let alone influence—the displacements made by the gas or any other substance inside, if I decide to move around, jump up and down, or stand still. By extension, since I am a free person and have the right to part with the substance at a time and place entirely at my discretion, **while retaining ownership of the substance until I formally surrender it**, the substance is also free to move in any direction I influence directly or indirectly, as long as third parties are not adversely affected by such movements.

This is an important principle that has a bearing on what we can do with **harmless** substances we produce in the course of a day. Note the emphasis on *harmless* here, as vomit and stool may contain bacteria and will be subject to numerous restrictions in terms of the applicability of PIPE. You can vomit in the forest because you are free, but not in people's carrot and orange smoothies. Farting, on the other hand, is completely harmless—well, most of the time, and I would argue that PIPE is always applicable to farting.

Let me repeat the line of reasoning:

1) People are free
2) People contain intestinal gases
3) People own their body excretions, waste and gases until they dispose of them or state clearly that they no longer claim them

Therefore, farts can move as freely as people, in any direction, any time.

The Five Characteristics of Free Farters

People who fart freely are different. In addition to the *Key Ideas* developed throughout this book, another key takeaway that you should remember and proudly advocate whenever possible is this list of characteristics of people who fart freely:

S	trong	You are mentally strong and in good health
T	ruthful	You tell things like they are and never circumvent the truth
I	ntegrity	You walk the talk. Sometimes, you walk and talk with your anus for each step, but that's not mandatory
N	atural	You behave naturally and probably also care for the environment
K	nowing	You know who you are, and you know yourself better than other people know themselves

Who would not like to be characterized by all these positive traits that many strive in vain to get associated to their names? By farting freely, you get a head start and can raise the ambition level on other fronts.

Situations Where You May Consider Not Farting—The Four Faux Farts

"If I am not allowed to fart in heaven, I don't want to go there."—
Fartin Luther

Funerals—Not that it's wrong or anything, but bear in mind that you may be mistaken for a recently deceased person and end up in a coffin before you know it. Many people would consider it disrespectful to fart at a funeral. True, there are moments of silence during a typical ceremony, so I understand why people would at least try to muffle the fart. But people should not stop living, and most dead people expect living people to do just that. So if you accept the risk of ending up in a coffin, you can fart silently at a funeral. If you think it's too risky, don't fart.

Fornication—Not that it's wrong or anything, but we need to be wary of the fact that most men cannot multi-task. It may divert attention, you lose focus, and the end result isn't as desired. Fart while making love, and your windsock may be left gasping for air in no time.

Faces—Not that it's wrong or anything, but they may be smoking, and the combustible gases may explode in his face or up your intestines. You risk getting sued, hospitalized or both. Also, you may hug or kiss the person seconds later, so just beware.

Fishing—Not that it's wrong or anything, but some farts are really loud and may scare the fish. I am not talking about your run-of-the-mill audible fart that we all produce at least once every day, I am talking Richter scale breaking gunshots that make people run for shelter and check their smart phones for breaking news on terrorist attacks. Granted, for some, this is a once-in-a-lifetime event that is not likely to coincide with the Catch of The Year, but why take chances? I am convinced that Jeremy Wade considers very carefully what to eat before and during his quests to land the various elusive River Monsters around the globe. Imagine that a single fart can ruin an entire TV show.

3.
How to Bring the Ideas in This Book to Life

Most books that claim that they can help you change your behavior for the better on a permanent basis, only contain text and fancy graphics to illustrate concepts rather than an actual toolkit that will take you beyond the nodding-in-agreement level. Reading about change without action is a waste of time. You are probably nodding in agreement now. Keep nodding—it gets better.

Embarking on a Journey to Become a Free Farter

Would you go anywhere important without a map? If you are walking through a wasteland fraught with dangers ranging from precipices to bottomless crevices, you wouldn't take a single step without knowing in which direction to start walking, right?

The journey to become a Free Farter may well be the most important journey of your life, and this book provides the map and the individual steps you need to take to reach the ideal end state.

To know how to get where you want to be, you need to know where you are. All people can be classified along two dimensions:

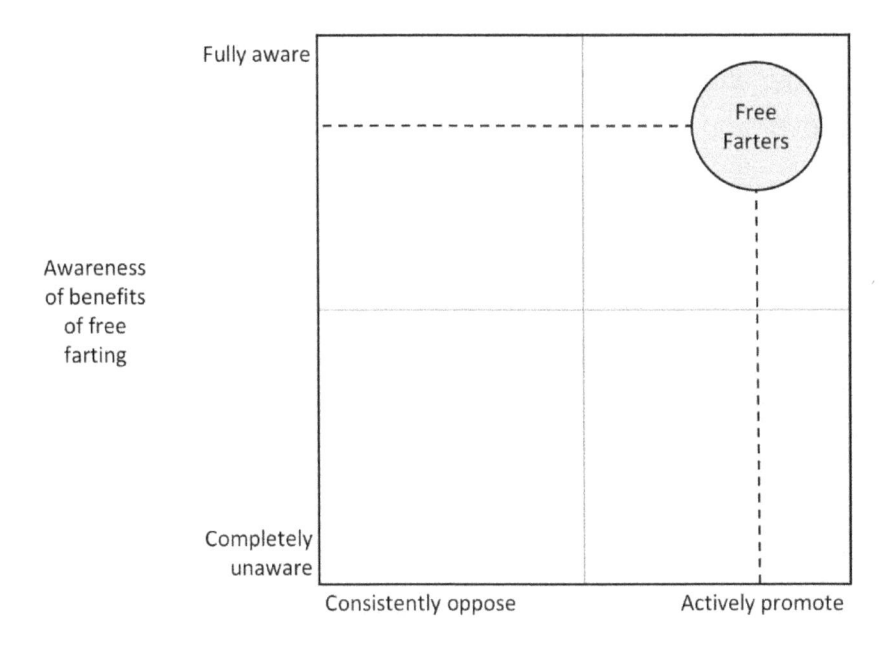

Figure 1

1) Awareness of benefits of free farting
2) Degree of support of free farting

Take the first dimension first. It's simple: you are somewhere in a continuum between **"Fully aware"** and **"Completely unaware"** of the physiological and spiritual benefits of free farting. If you are fully aware, then you know all the health benefits of farting, and you acknowledge that farting freely is beneficial for your mental health. If you are completely unaware, on the other hand, you believe farting is a disease that should be cured at all cost, and probably have no idea why we even need to go to the bathroom and sit down once a day. The other dimension is also fairly straightforward. You support and promote free farting whenever you can, or you consistently oppose free farting, almost as vehemently as Aunt Mildred. Most likely, you are—like most people—somewhere between the two.

To become a Free Farter, you obviously need to be **fully aware** of the benefits of free farting AND **actively promote free farting** whenever you can, through words and deeds.

This will effectively put you in the upper right-hand quadrant in the classification framework (Figure 1).

Although each and every one of us could be anywhere on the chart in Figure 2, those who do not qualify as Free Farters generally fall into four broad categories:

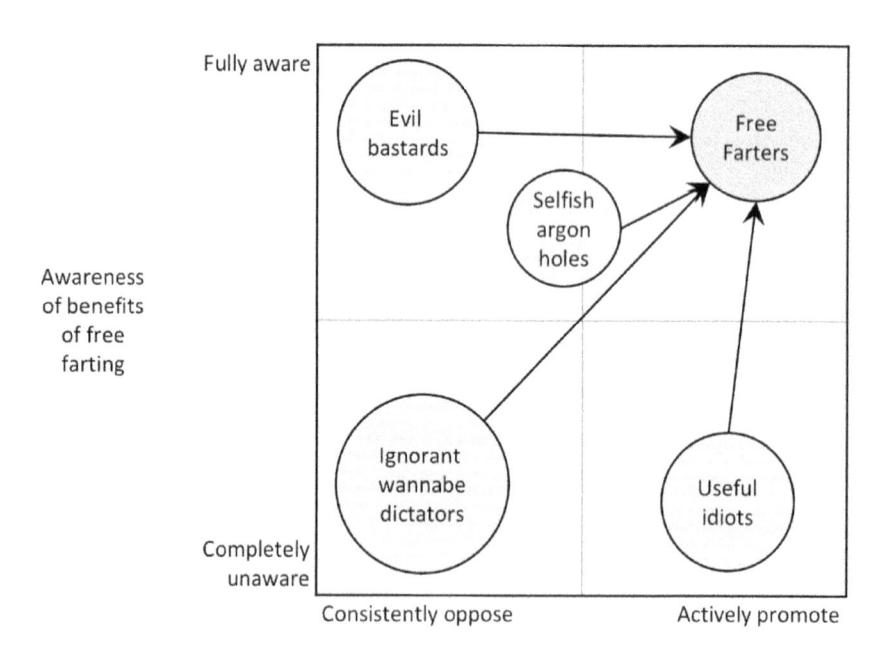

Figure 2: Broad categorization and ideal path to Free Farter

Evil bastards—those who are highly aware of the benefits of free farting but consistently oppose it. Opposing good is promoting bad. Simple as that. I will cover this in more detail in a later chapter.

Selfish argon holes—those who are well aware of the benefits of farting freely but do not practice it. Instead, they fart only when alone or when they know that their fart is odorless like argon. They are too selfish to risk making fools of themselves publicly in the name of progress.

Ignorant wannabe dictators—those who have no idea about the benefits of free farting and oppose it without any justification.

Useful idiots—those who know nothing about why farting is good for you but promote free farting as a matter of principle.

Obviously, people may find themselves anywhere in the four quadrants, including stuck in the middle or in the sinister Zone of Eternal Constipation.

From each broad category, there is an ideal, straight-line trajectory to the elevated state of Free Farter. Should you opt to close this book and try to go down the path to illumination without the guidance this book provides, you do so at your peril. You risk many horrid outcomes, notably the ones illustrated below (starting from an arbitrarily selected position for illustration purposes only):

Spiraling into mediocrity (Figure 3)
A drunkard's walk (Figure 4)
Getting trapped in the zone of eternal constipation (Figure 5)
Rampant indecisiveness (Figure 6)

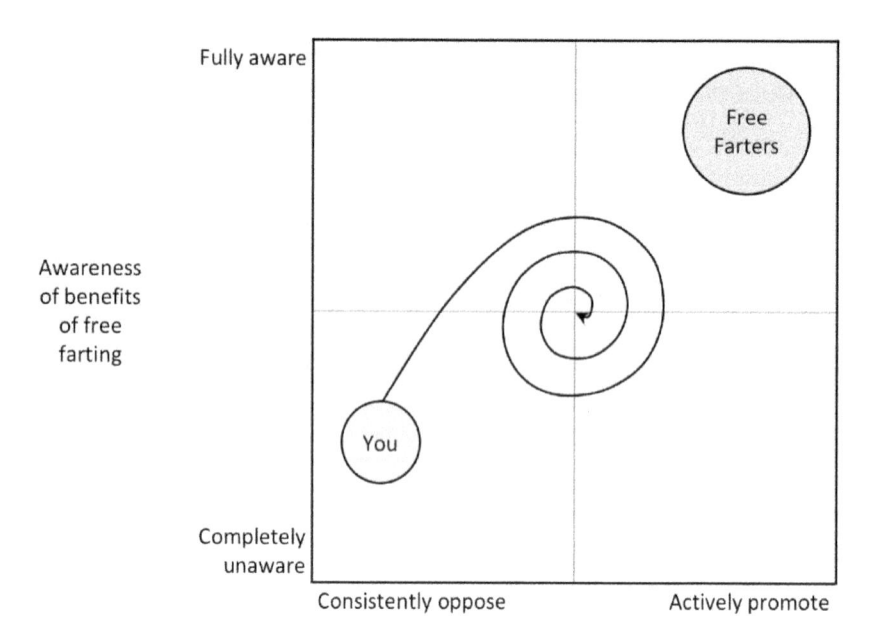

Figure 3: Spiraling into mediocrity

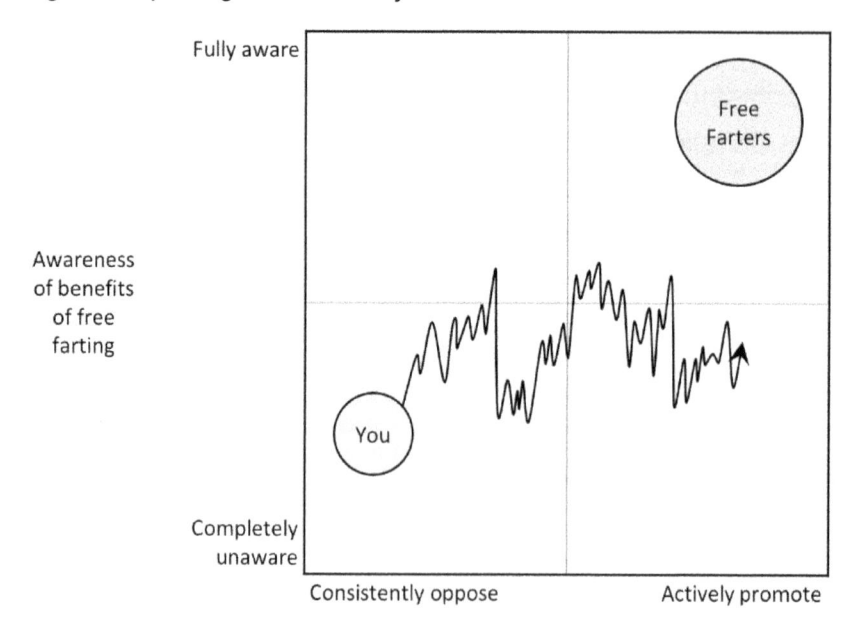

Figure 4: A drunkard's walk

~ 34 ~

WARNING: the perimeter around the **Zone of Eternal Constipation** is one-way only. There is **NO WAY OUT**. Also, there are no warnings as you approach it, a bit like Earth's gravitational field or the event horizon surrounding black holes. All of a sudden you find yourself incapable of achieving orbit escape velocity and your fate is sealed. Luckily, by following the steps described in detail in this book, you can't go wrong.

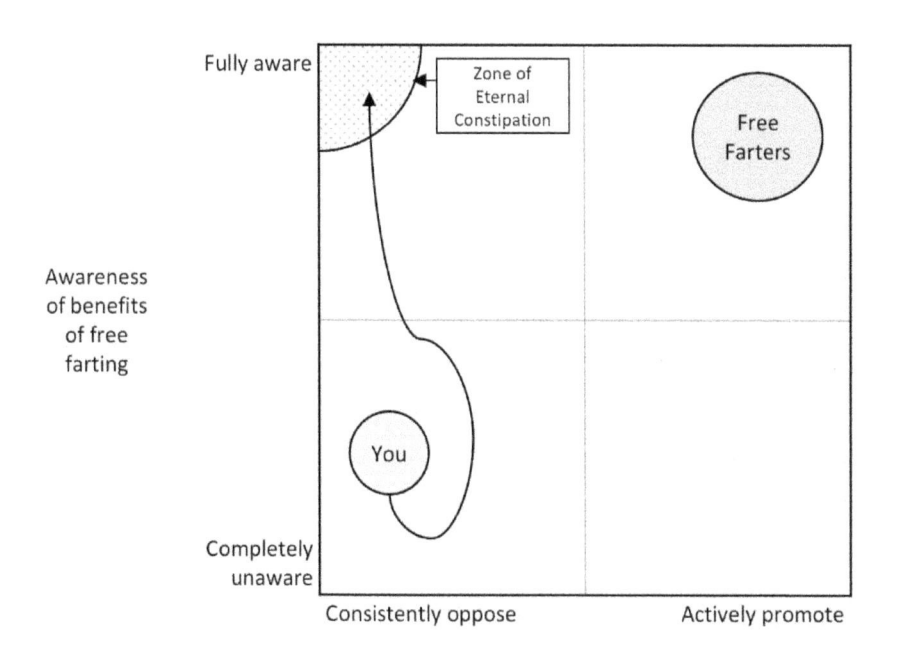

Figure 5: Trapped in the zone of eternal constipation

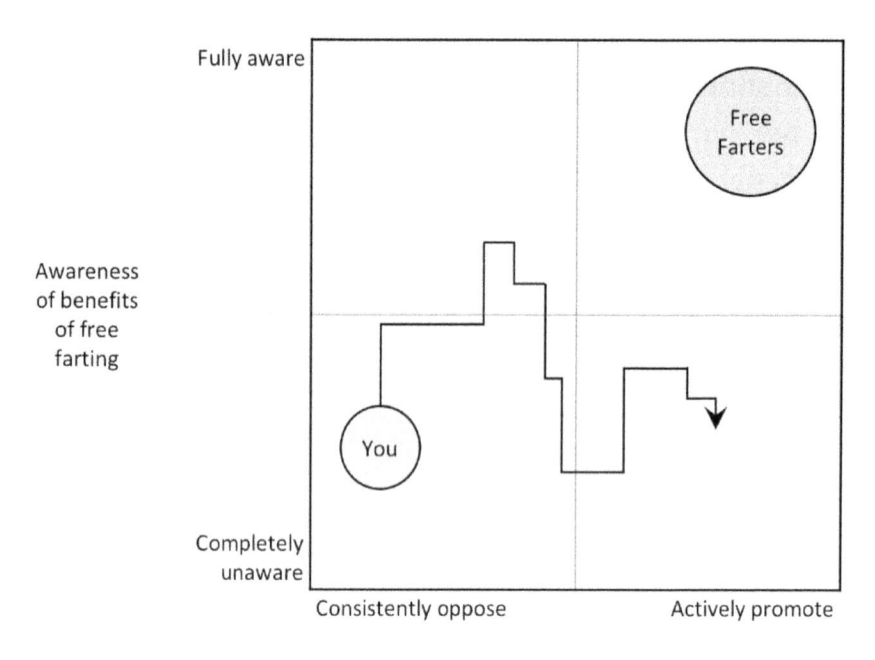

Figure 6: Rampant indecisiveness

What does this mean for you? It means you should think long and hard about what kind of person you are, i.e. in which category you fall. The answer is inside you, and possibly on its way out as we speak. Depending on the category, your focus should be on awareness building and behaviors described in each step as follows:

CATEGORY	AWARENESS BUILDING	BEHAVIORS
Evil bastards	*Key Idea # 8: People who tell you to stop farting are evil*	All
Selfish argon holes	Step 1—Everybody knows that everybody farts, including The Emperor Step 2—Fart because it is good for you *Key Idea # 3: People who deliberately fart alone are selfish* *Key Idea # 5: If in doubt whether you should fart, ask yourself, "Would a dog fart here?"*	All
Ignorant wannabe dictators	All, with special attention to: *Key Idea # 1: Believing that celebrities and politicians don't fart is a threat to democracy* *Key Idea # 7: Freedom is natural, never forced*	All
Useful idiots	Step 1: Everybody knows that everybody farts, including The Emperor Step 2: Fart because it is good for you Step 3: Look to Man's Best Friend *Key Idea # 2: With robots taking over, farting may be our only hope if we are to survive as a species* *Key Idea # 4: Farting may help you financially* *Key Idea # 6: Farting can help you find a suitable partner to procreate with*	Keep up the good work, but go through all steps to sharpen your ability to promote free farting

Table 1: Focus areas for each category of non-Free Farters

Note that the above table lists proposed focus areas to guide you in your journey—it does not mean you can skip a step!

Spiritual Freedom as a Continuous Result of a Virtuous Circle

Spiritual freedom—or any kind of freedom for that matter—is not achieved as a result of a single, one-time effort. Rather, it is an outcome of a continual drive to attain the highest state of enlightenment or other personal or professional achievement, with a continual feedback loop based on intermittent achievements.

The process of farting yourself to spiritual freedom is best described as a simple yet powerful feedback loop (Figure 7) that starts with the acknowledgement that you **FEEL** an urge to accomplish something. When the urge becomes strong enough, your body and mind will work in tandem and initiate action. In our specific case, the urge initially manifests itself as the need to fart, or at least a feeling of intestinal pressure. Sometimes you don't even realize that you need to fart, but you feel a physiological imbalance that is unsustainable in the short term. Your body and soul interpret the signal and mobilize for action. At this point, you as a reader will have understood that the physical urge is a sign of a drive to make a sacrifice for a greater cause, meaning that you are ready to embarrass yourself to achieve more freedom for yourself and other members of mankind. To be clear, the assertion that you embarrass yourself by farting is based on observed mainstream reactions by people who see constipation as the highest level of enlightenment. In case you haven't noticed, there are quite few of them around.

Once the urge has been identified and acknowledged—and even if you haven't yet understood the full reach of your sentiment and the actions you are about to take—you will instinctively **ACT**, i.e. complete the task your body and soul requested you to. This is obviously the easy part, and constitutes a simple fart, or a few farts in succession. Duration, sound and smell do not matter here, even if it is essential that other people (especially authority, cf. Step 6) notice your actions. If, over time, nobody notices what you do, how can you be free? Other people's reactions are **not** the main driver here; the point is that you fart without caring what people say.

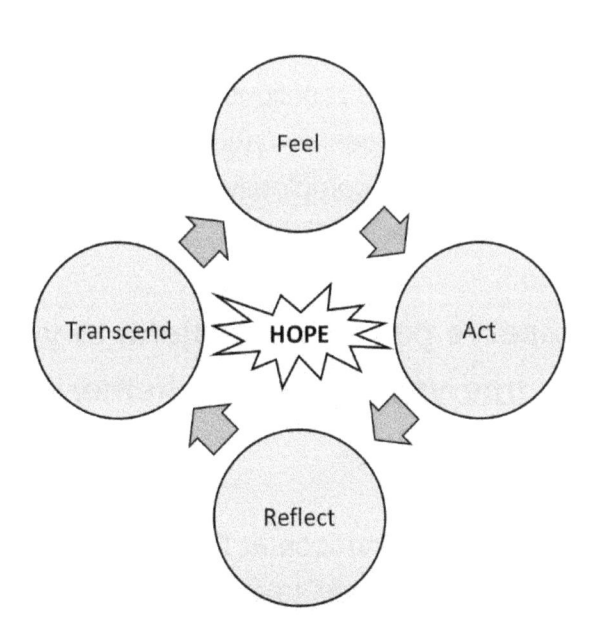

Figure 7: The powerful F-A-R-T positive feedback loop

Will you necessarily be free once you have farted with other people around you? Obviously not. People may think you lost control for a second, and forget about it, especially if you excuse yourself. Also, other people's reactions are of secondary importance. The question is whether you act the way you act because you know deep down you don't care about what other people think. Therefore, you need to **REFLECT** over the events that have unfolded and how you feel. You are only free when you don't even consider for a second how you will be perceived as a person when you fart audibly.

When you have assessed the overall outcome of your actions and other people's reactions, you may be ready to **TRANSCEND** to the next level of freedom and enlightenment. This affirmation, in turn, will trigger new feelings, and subsequent actions (farts) required to attain the next level of freedom, which, again, must be reflected over before transcending to the following level. Again, the point is not how or whether people react; the point is that you notice reactions and you ignore the reactions. Whether they laugh, point, jeer or call you names, it doesn't matter. What matters is that you see reactions, and you are completely oblivious to them. This is a critical point that should be highlighted:

You only observe people's reactions to your farts <u>to assess how free you feel</u>—not whether people start condoning your farting.

Let's pause for a minute and look at the word "transcend", which may sound mystical or "esoteric" to some. It simply means to move to a higher level or go beyond a threshold such as a border. Now, incidentally, *transcendental meditation* has been around for decades and incited Westerners to adopt oriental attitudes to life. An authoritative website describes the word "transcending" as— among other things, 'achieving inner happiness and improved self-confidence'—*being yourself.* My point all along: we should be who we are. It doesn't get better than that.

What is the role of HOPE in this process? You may answer that it all revolves around HOPE, but what does that mean?

To answer that question, we need to turn to the famous Dutch philosopher, Spinoza, who said that *"a free people is led more by hope than by fear."* This idea applies to actions we take in everyday life, including the use of our bodily functions such as farting. Free people should not be put in situations where they first need to think through whether their actions are allowed, meaning they should not fear. But alas, when we fart, we fear. We fear being vilified, reprimanded, ostracized, ridiculed, talked about behind our backs, ignored, demoted, and generally being classified as lower-class individuals.

A Truly Free Person will not fall into this trap. He or she will think:

- "I hope it's OK for people if I fart here", not, "Will someone punch me in the gut if I fart?".

- "I hope people respect me for who I am regardless of whether I happen to fart", not, "Oh, no, I farted. I just lost all respect and probably their friendship too!".

- "I hope they recognize all people's physical needs", not, "I will never get this job now—might as well leave the interview!".

To paraphrase Spinoza, only when hope supplants fear as the primary emotion preceding our actions, can we be truly free.

Now try to consider how the feedback loop would work—if at all—should your behavior be driven by **FEAR**. In this scenario, you will have FEAR replacing hope in the middle. The first **FEELING** will be followed by a **SUPPRESSED** action due to FEAR of the consequences. This subsequently leads to a sense of **CONFINEMENT** (Figure 8).

Effectively, rather than a virtuous circle with a self-reinforcing positive effect, **the feedback loop will be permanently short-circuited and bypass the critical REFLECT step**, and your behavior will be driven by instinct which will successively become more primitive and as far from free-spirited as possible. We are now in the realm of humans' "state of nature", as described by the 17th-century English philosopher Thomas Hobbes in his famous book *Leviathan*. In probably the most-cited passage, Hobbes lists many negative aspects of the state of nature, the worst being the

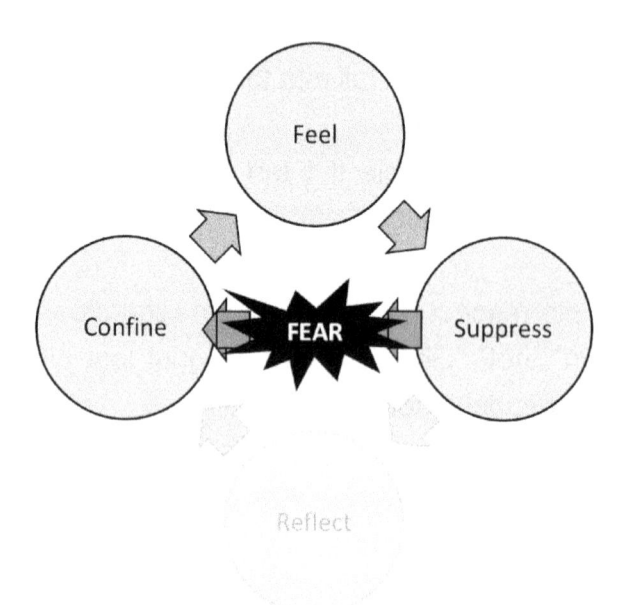

Figure 8: A positive feedback loop short-circuited by fear

"*continual fear and danger of violent death*". Clearly, he alludes to fear of being impaled or disemboweled for farting in the wrong moment. This fear is still part of human nature, even if pillorying replaced impaling over the centuries, and slandering on social media replaced pillorying quite recently.

The state of nature is the "*war of every man against every man,*" which is a consequence of every man's right to do everything, even to other people, which, in turn, makes security impossible. According to Hobbes' second law of nature, people will voluntarily give up their liberty to do everything—including fart freely—in order to achieve security and peace, provided that all others do the same.

In today's almost civilized world, we are luckily beyond debating whether it is acceptable to pound a spiked bludgeon into a person's head just because they stole the boar roast off your skewer, so the social contract is already in place, but far from perfect. Somewhere, somehow, things went terribly wrong, and there was a tacit agreement among most people that we shouldn't fart in other people's presence. I get throat-slitting, keelhauling, rape, theft, arson and numerous other bad behaviors some unlucky people still fall victim to. Let's agree that it's bad, and let's find practical jokes to resort to when we dislike one another. But farting? What needs to be added to the Hobbesian social contract is the **general and unconditional acceptance of farting** (along with a few other, relatively minor things).

How to Make the Positive Feedback Loop Work in Real Life

As you may imagine, the four-step process and associated urge, as well as hope as the driving force behind all our actions as Truly Free People, is not specific to farting. We feel urges dozens of times in the course of a day and tens of thousands of times in a lifetime. You can apply it to other urges too. Complete this exercise before reading on:

Based on the example "Freedom to swear", list three potentially controversial or—according to most people's point of view—slightly offensive actions that, if repeated multiple times, will lead to new freedom or reinforce existing freedoms (Table 2).

	Freedom to swear	Feedback loop 1	Feedback loop 2	Feedback loop 3 etc.
Feel	Feel anger and urge to swear	Based on the hesitant response to my expressed freedom, I now feel that...		
<u>Act</u> (underlined)	<u>Swear</u> out loud so old ladies hear me	<u>Swear</u> in new setting to pave way for extended freedom		
Reflect	Newfound but hitherto suppressed freedom to express my true feelings	(Your notes here)	*SAMPLE – DO NOT WRITE HERE*	
Transcend	My freedom to express my true feelings has gained little understanding by those around me, which makes me feel uneasy	(Your notes here)		

Table 2: Actions and feelings log to be used for Steps 2-7

Now let's get specific and practical. What you need to do is the following:

1. Record Actions and Feelings

For each step 2-7 in this book (step 1 is a step of reflection), fill in a table with a minimum of three cycles FEEL-ACT-REFLECT-TRANSCEND. For your convenience, I have appended an empty table at the end of each chapter. (Other authors try to sell you additional "workbooks" to help you achieve your goal. For the record, I would never even consider exploiting people in bad situations for my own financial benefit. It's simply unheard of.)

2. Track Progress Towards a Defined Target

To keep track of progress, use the table supplied at the end of each chapter, and fill in between one and three plus (+) or minus (-) signs based on the magnitude and significance of each step in a cycle. Keep a tally of your overall score by adding up the pluses and subtracting the minuses. Let's say your feeling prior to the first fart gets a FEEL score of 3 pluses because the urge is completely natural and you feel no inhibitions, the ACT of farting itself gets a score of 2 due to a fairly high volume and a setting in which your spiritual freedom will be tested, but you REFLECT and realize that the actual sense of freedom attained is a minus 1, and your ability to TRANSCEND to the next level of freedom is also a minus 1, then your event score is 3 (3 plus 2 minus 1 minus 1). When the pluses outnumber the minuses by a target number you must set yourself, you have effectively reached a satisfactory level of spiritual freedom and shaken off the shackles of pseudo-civilization.

	1	2	3	4	5	6	7	8
Feel	+++	++						
Act	++	+++						
Reflect	-	+						
Transcend	-	-						
Total +	5	6						
Total -	2	1						
Event score	3	5						
Running total +	3	8						

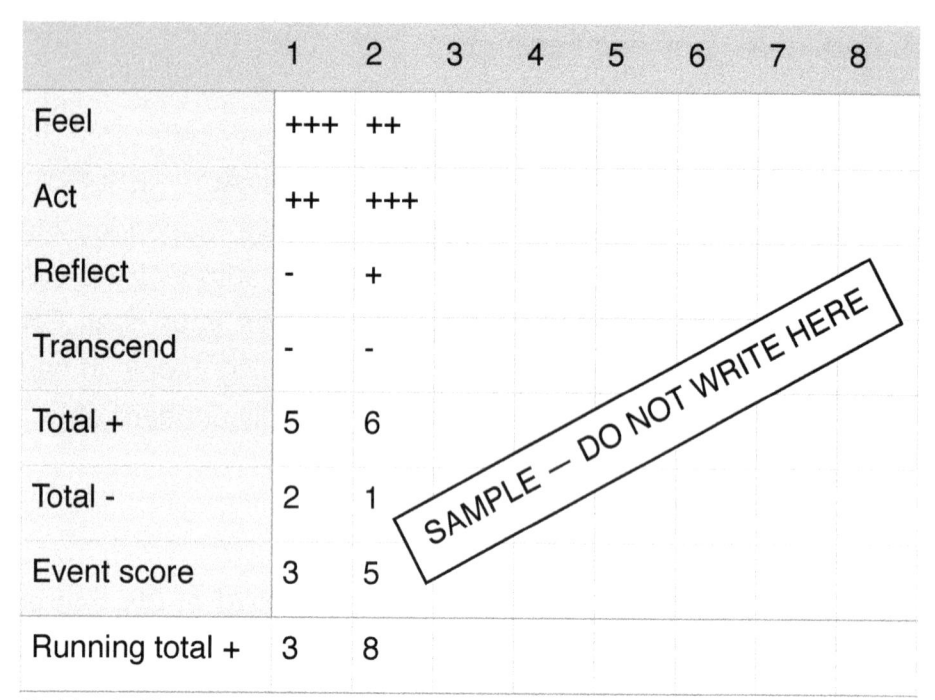

Table 3: Progress tracker with sample scores

From my own personal experience, the number you should aim for is **42**. Those with an interest in oriental mythology can aim for **108**, which is calculated as 42 + 24 + 42 again.

Do not fall into the trap of extrapolating the first couple of scores and predict the total number of feedback cycles you need to go through. In the above example, you have an average score of 4 over two cycles (5 + 3 divided by 2), which may lead you to conclude that you will be done in 42/4 = 10.5 cycles. Then you just need to fart 11 times, reflect a little, and then you are a Free Farter and a Truly Free Person, right? **Absolutely not.**

I guarantee you that this will be a journey that will resemble a roller coaster ride at times. You will have cycles with all negative scores, you may even have a negative running total on more than one occasion, and you will definitely feel like giving up many times because of repeated setbacks. There are no shortcuts here. As always, discipline and hard work are essential ingredients for success.

4.
Step 1: Acknowledge That We Are Human Beings and Prepare to Subvert Against the Robots

"Intelligence is based on how efficient a species became at doing the things they need to survive."—Chuck Darnwind

Since time immemorial, humans have farted in the jungle, in the desert, on the savannah of East Africa, in Carthage, Sparta, Frankfurt and London, Ontario. Numerous physical traits and behaviors have developed over time: canine teeth are smaller now because we cook food and tell people to get lost rather than baring our teeth, and our tail is simply a small bone at the end of the spine rather than a proper tail, now that we only climb trees for fun. There is even a theory that women developed breasts as a replacement for the attractive but less visible rear end as we stood erect. Nobody knows with certainty what function our appendix has, and tonsils were once believed to be remnants of gills—what fish use to extract oxygen from water. Apparently, we develop and move slowly but surely towards perfection. Has anything happened to farting? No evidence suggests that. If it ain't broke, don't fix it. Farting is here to stay.

In addition to war, pestilence, water shortage, undernourishment and global warming, we are now facing another problem that has the potential to eradicate civilization as we know it. Although humans will continue to exist on the planet for centuries and millennia to come, robots are slowly but surely taking over. They drive subway trains, they assemble cars, and they even drive them for some of us. They trade shares on the stock exchange for us, and they vacuum our floors. Granted, some of these automated devices aren't robots as we picture them from 1950s sci-fi movies or The Wizard of Oz, with bulky arms and legs, barely able to walk a step without using all its computing power, let alone pick up a glass without breaking it. But they are robots, and they are taking over! It's even more worrisome to know that a robot can take any shape or form, assemble a new robot, and make the stock market crash. Not only will they steal our jobs—they will also eradicate our college savings and our pensions. Folks, we are being invaded by an enemy who may look like just about anything and hide inside any gadget we use in our daily lives. If you are reading this book on a tablet computer, you may unwittingly host a top brass robot strategy meeting as we are sitting here farting and getting our pensions wiped out!

Clearly, machines taking over for humans is not a new phenomenon. Most people consider the Industrial Revolution epitomized by the spinning jenny as a watershed in the history of the man-machine relationship. However, it is a little-known historical fact that it all began in Ireland probably a century or two earlier, when bagpipers started to replace professional farters—the highly skilled *braigetoír* mentioned earlier—who performed at various events, accompanied by background musicians. As documented in The Image of Irelande, bagpipes were primarily used for military purposes at least until the 16th century. Today, they are used solely as musical instruments, and the once-proud *braigetoír* trade is all but forgotten. Historians estimate that one bagpiper could deprive as many as eight breadwinning *braigetoír* of gainful employment. We can only imagine the hardship suffered by the hundreds—possibly even thousands—of penniless flatulists scouring town and countryside for work, willing to swallow their pride and accept the most demeaning day job. The day the last hairy-butted *braigetoír* was told to stop farting, pull his trousers back up, and look for work elsewhere was indeed a sad day in human history.

Facing this threat which is no longer a threat but reality, it's good to be human, with individual thoughts, flaws and various biological processes—some appealing, some not so appealing.

In the not so distant future, when robots have demoted us to second-class citizens and restricted all communication between humans, we may be left with body scents as the only viable means of communication. It will start slowly, when humans pass each other on the street among humanoids who look like us, we discreetly fart to identify each other as fellow tribesmen subjugated by the same enemy. Eventually, we will develop ways to generate different scents with different meanings, when used in combination with length and frequency.

Because farting is frowned upon today and is likely to be considered rude in the future (unless the most influential bloggers read this book and live by its principles), the first few attempts to communicate through body scents will probably rely on odor from armpits. They are almost bound to fail miserably, as they are likely to go along these examples:

- "Hi, I'm Hugo Boss."

- "Hi, what a coincidence, I'm also Hugo Boss."

- "Wait, was that Gabriela Sabatini?"

Or:

- "Hi, I'm Hugo Boss."

- "Hi, I'm Ralph Lauren."

- "You stink, get lost!"

So, body odor is a dead end as a means of communication between humans oppressed by robots. What about foot odor? Impractical, as you would have to take your shoes off every time you meet someone you believe to be human. You simply wouldn't have the time, and undercover humanoid robot cops would immediately get suspicious if a significant part of the population would all of a sudden stop to take their shoes off every so often.

This is where farting comes in. Smoke signals—and Morse, for that matter—will have been long forgotten by then, but the idea is the same. Duration, frequency and color (meaning chemical composition) will all be used to construct words and sentences. Of course, the first few conversations will be short, simple and to the point, although the intended message will probably be left hanging in midair (no pun intended, I swear!):

- "I am human. I had eggs for breakfast."

- "I am human too. I also had eggs for breakfast. They may have been a bit off."

- "Well, smell you then."

- "Smell you."

Much like smoke signals and HTML used in web page design, the language will develop over time, allowing us to have conversations and meetings like today. Dialects and regional languages will develop due to dietary differences, and a need for interpreters will arise, especially if, for instance, the resistance movement in Europe joins forces with their Asian counterparts and plan a coordinated rebellion against the robots. The knowledge of regional languages, or *Fartois*, will be disseminated at underground universities.

If we are to stand a chance against an invisible enemy, we need to preserve the ability to fart and under no circumstances suppress it, as over time, robots will learn how to look, behave and smell like humans.

With robots taking over nearly every aspect of human life—and eventually the entire planet—farting may be our only hope if we are to survive as a species
(Key Idea # 2)

Will that mean that we cannot even use farting as a secure means of communication? We cannot avoid this risk entirely, but I firmly believe that evolution will work in our favor. How? Think about large collections of birds, such as penguins—with colonies that may count tens of thousands, how does a couple recognize each other after a fishing trip? They manage to identify each other through the sound of thousands of bickering couples—and the smell from enormous amounts of guano. In fact, penguin guano is visible from space, and satellite imagery of penguin excrements is used to estimate their population size and composition! Space!

Imagine the conversation between a penguin couple if they somehow managed to read on the winternet that not only the size of the guano, but also the color and density are possible to view and analyze from space.

Male penguin: "Honey, it says on the winternet that our guano is visible from space!"
Female penguin: "What! Now what did you do? I told you not to go to that fermented herring party with those irresponsible friends of yours, who hardly ever bother to look for rocks before the nesting season. It always ends like this!"

Call me childish, but I would be proud if my turds were visible from space. I would go as far as to say that I would be happy if that was my only achievement in life. I can see myself smiling on my deathbed, forgetting completely that I never became a movie star, a famous author or a Wall Street tycoon. I would be mumbling to myself with my closest family around my bed: "Visible from space... Used in satellite imagery..." My family would of course think that I had lost it and my passing would be long overdue. They would each split my estate mentally and imagine what they would do with their part. "Maybe a trip to the Antarctica? I heard penguin colonies are impressive sights, but very noisy and smelly because of all that guano. Maybe Mauritius is a better choice? How much is the copyright of that silly, juvenile book he wrote? Probably nothing. Is he gone yet?"

My point is that, even if penguins all look the same and literally spray each other in guano all day long, and the noise is unbearable, evolution has made sure mates will find each other. Consequently, even if robots should succeed in emulating human behavior in all respects, evolution will work in our favor, and humans will also be able to identify one another amongst malicious *doppelgängers*. In the same way as antelopes develop speed and agility that enable them to escape voracious big cats and hyenas, humans will develop new skills to avoid captivation by robots. Our sense of smell will become more acute for each generation, and we will be able to distinguish between a robot's electronically generated smells and authentic, truly organic smells that humans generate. Not only that, but we will also be able to control our anuses like skunks target the spray they excrete from their anal glands. Ironically, as civilization progresses and produces the most advanced machines ever made, we turn towards the animal kingdom to protect ourselves from being made extinct.

Take sound as another example. Smelling the difference between a human fart and an electronically generated robot fart is like hearing the difference between compressed sound and lossless sound when listening to digital music, of—for those of my age or older—the difference between vinyl and CDs. When the first CD was produced and sold to the mass market, trained ears called the CD sound "robot sound". There you go.

Surely, not all of us will make it. It's sad, but that's how evolution works. Those who survive will produce stronger and smarter offspring—a self-reinforcing effect.

> **Key attitudes and behaviors to remember from Step 1:**
>
> - Humans have probably always farted and will continue to do so because it works
> - Robots will take over the world and we must be prepared to revolt against them, using farting as a secret language

5.
Step 2: Fart Because It's Good for You

"The best cure for a body is a quiet fart." —Napoleon Bonafarte

This step is so logical that it shouldn't be necessary to explain it. If it doesn't feel good or do us any good, then the body function wouldn't have evolved in the first place. Simple as that. This shouldn't be confused with the idea that if it feels good, it must be good for you. If that was the case, then many drugs should be legalized.

Before we look at how farting benefits your health, let's consider what happens if you don't fart. A disturbing fact about farts is that a couple of the intestinal gases are flammable. If we don't fart, we expose ourselves to spontaneous human combustion. Search for it on the internet. I guarantee you will want to avoid it for yourself and your family and friends.

Now consider what you expose other people to if you expect them not to fart, and even tell them openly to stop farting. Effectively, you are telling them to keep accumulating flammable gases inside them. Say what? Would you **ever** utter those words? Unless you are a ruthless drug lord in the middle of an all-out war with a competing organization, you wouldn't, right?

Farting is actually good for you in a number of surprising ways, according to an article found on the news websites The Host Puffing Tons and The Windia Times.

Farting alleviates bloating. We all experience a bloated stomach from time to time, and reasons vary. Overeating is one. In addition to eating less, which many of us probably should, you can also eat more slowly to avoid bloating. Gas build-up is another completely natural cause of bloating. Bloating doesn't normally pose a serious threat to your health, but who wants to look and feel fatter than they are? Whatever the reason for a bloated stomach is, there is a simple and effective remedy: farting. Holding the fart back, on the other hand, keeps you bloated. Why am I even writing this? It's obvious. **You. Need. To. Fart.**

Farting relieves stomach pain. In case gas build-up causes pain, there is no better way to relieve that pain than by farting. While most of us know from experience that holding gas may cause pain, there are other, more serious consequences for your health. A group of Danish medical experts claim to have evidence that keeping your gas inside you can lead to complications like bloating, indigestion, and heartburn—especially on long-haul flights, due to pressurized cabins. What does that mean? That if there is one place where you should fart, it's inside an aircraft. It's also pretty safe from a retaliation point of view: who would yell at you or punch you in the gut in the air in this day and age, knowing that they would face a long prison sentence, with nasty smells being the least of their worries?

Farting can prevent damage to your colon. Another negative health effect of holding your fart in, is potential damage to your colon. If you have hemorrhoids, they may flare up, especially if your colon is already in an unhealthy condition. Again, the solution is simple: fart when needed. If you don't, your health problems will worsen and maybe even multiply. Do not **under any circumstances** consider this choosing the lesser of two evils. Farting is good for you, like breathing. Would you stop breathing for fear of depriving other people of oxygen? I didn't think so.

Believe it or not, but **inhaling your fart can reduce the risk of disease**. There is a compound called hydrogen sulfide, which is produced in small quantities in our bowels and emitted along with other gases when we fart. If inhaled, it can protect us against heart diseases and arthritis, according to a study published in the journal Medicinal Chemistry Communications. Should you, as a caring individual, share this particular benefit of farting with those near and dear, and even colleagues and passersby? Of course! If you didn't, you would be selfish, right?

People who deliberately fart alone are selfish
(Key Idea # 3)

In fact, if you feel that a fart is coming, you should either move closer to people or let them know a health salvo is coming. You can yell, "**Everybody over here! Free disease protection, limited-time offer only! First come, first served! No needles, no side effects!**"

This can pan out in a number of ways, so you must be mentally prepared for a variety of outcomes.

First of all, you need to look at the map. Where are you? More specifically, in which country are you? This is important in order to assess the probability of being attacked if you willfully fart close to strangers. We are talking about countries with a higher density of people carrying the WARRIOR GENE. According to scientific research, "individuals with the so-called 'warrior gene' display higher levels of aggression in response to provocation." In the experiment referred to, test persons were asked to hurt a person they believed had taken money from them by administering varying amounts of hot sauce. The warrior gene is simply a slightly defective anger-soothing enzyme regulator in the brain, and is more prevalent in the populations in "warrior nations" like the United States, the United Kingdom, Germany, Finland, and Japan.

In plain English: you may wish to go to Scandinavia or Tibet to try farting in public on purpose the first time. People there are less likely to beat you up. If you can't afford the trip and need to stay in a warrior nation, buy a pair of decent running shoes and take up jogging a few weeks in advance. I heard it's almost as healthy as farting.

Once you have made up your mind to share the benefits of a smelly fart with strangers, you need to think about how to react in the following scenarios:

1) People move further away from you due to a general apprehension towards loud strangers

2) People are listening to music and won't even notice you

3) Only a gray-haired, middle-aged woman with home-knit clothes and beads in her hair will pay attention, aside from two Japanese tourists who capture it all on video

4) You get arrested for false marketing claims. To prepare for this scenario, I recommend that you read *Step 6—Fart in The Presence of Authority*, section "**The Judge**"

5) You fart and get beaten up by a leather-clad motorcyclist, and the Japanese tourists capture it on video

6) You fart, and there is no smell, and people shrug their shoulders and think, "Another con artist…"

As it happens, the substance that protects against arthritis and cardio-vascular diseases is also the one that results in smelly farts, so try to make sure you can deliver the goods if you attract a crowd eager to benefit from pain-free disease prevention. If not, the old feathers and bucket of tar will not be far away. And should they opt for pillorying in a bout of nostalgia, the last thing the enraged villagers will do is... fart on you. Maybe kids and the odd drunkard passing by at night will fart on you, but only because they don't know that they should save the good stuff for their families. Make sure you have sniffed enough farts in advance to reduce the effects of worsened arthritis if you end up pilloried for many days in cold weather.

Farting can help you determine whether you have food allergies, such as lactose and gluten intolerance, which tend to make you fart excessively. We, as actual or aspiring Free Farters, know that this is not a problem in itself, but if you do fart a lot after consuming certain foods, you should get tested for allergies. What's a lot in this context? I reckon 20,000 times or more per day should warrant an allergy test, but that's entirely up to you. If there is a constant fog around you, that's probably an indication that something odd is going on in your bowels. Or maybe you should have your eyesight checked.

Farting can tell you whether you have a healthy diet and whether you need to make adjustments. If you hardly ever fart, you probably don't get enough fiber; if you fart a lot without odor, you probably consume too much carbohydrates; and if your farts smell awful most of the time, you probably eat too much red meat. If you fart a lot AND it smells bad, your alternating days pizza/hamburger diet of the average bachelor is working wonders. Trust me, I have been there.

People who fart a lot are healthier. Why? Because healthy, leafy vegetables like cauliflower and cabbage feed the good bacteria we all have in our stomachs and that improve our digestion. Now that gives me a bad conscience. For years, I starved those poor defenseless little things, and probably shortened the time I get to spend with my grandchildren. On top of that, I contributed to food and water shortage because red meat requires more animal feed and more water to produce than any other food item, AND I kept methane-belching livestock alive long enough to trigger global warming. At least the cows and bulls I ate are dead now and don't spew out hundreds of gallons of greenhouse gases every day. Actually, that makes me a hero, right?

Farting keeps you physically active. Nowadays, where people spend hours on end in front of their computers at work, watch movies on their tablets at home, and prefer elevators to stairs and Segways to walking, any physical movement is beneficial to your health. Farters move—or make other people move—in many ways:

When you or someone else farts a particularly smelly one, you move away from the stench, and sometimes walk a few feet to open a window.

You tilt sideways because it makes farting easier. Remember to vary the tilt by alternating between left and right, and between a full sideways tilt with a straight spine and a simple buttock lift.

You wave off the smell with your hand, sometimes frantically. This is particularly beneficial for those who use a computer mouse at work.

There are numerous yoga poses that will specifically induce farting and improve your digestion in general, including the Wind-Relieving pose called *Pawanmuktasana*. Unbeknownst to the public and yoga practitioners across the globe, yoga was invented and introduced to Western visitors (mostly invaders after Marco Polo) because Indians and other Asians found Westerners so constipated that something had to be done. Historians have yet to trace the course of events, but preliminary findings indicate that the locals quickly made up a thousand-year-old tradition based on an accidental discovery that certain body poses are good for your bowels. A conversation between two frustrated South Asians a few hundred years back may have gone along these lines:

- "Sanjay, can you make them sit like you did the other day, when you farted like crazy? Ask the old wise guy on that hilltop to come up with some ancient names and a story to tell them, those stuck-up pale-faces. I'm sure they'll swallow it hook, line and sinker."

- "Sure thing, Kumar, I'm on it. I agree, this can't go on."

Farting can speed up diagnosis when you have a stomach pain. According to numerous medicine websites such as emedicinehealth.com, flatulence may cause pain and discomfort: "Some people have pain when gas is present in the intestine. When pain is on the left side of the colon, it can be confused with heart disease. When the pain is on the right side of the colon, it may mimic gallstones or appendicitis."

So, if the problem is the presence of gas in the intestine, get rid of it. For your own health: fart, and avoid misdiagnosis and all the possible sinister outcomes that line up in their wake. Fart a lot to be on the safe side. You do not want to have people cut you open just because you want to avoid farting. Surgeons have knives, for crying out loud! Think of all the blood, the stitches, the scars, the medical follow-up after the operation, the frustration, the battle with insurance companies, being replaced at work because nobody expects you to pull through—the consequences of not farting may be formidable. Not only do you stay healthy through farting when required, but there are financial benefits, too. As a farter, you can ask for sworn testimonies from people around you and ask for a discount on your health insurance because of a higher probability of a correct diagnosis if you have an undefined ailment.

Farting may help you financially
(Key Idea # 4)

Let's take this last one a bit further: we are now beyond the realm of personal benefits of farting—we are talking potentially enormous benefits to society as a whole. I hereby call upon the Surgeon General in all countries to make farting mandatory in order to employ scarce health resources more optimally, especially in the light of an aging population in most Western countries, Japan and South Korea. Likewise, medical schools world-wide should consider shortening degree programs because physicians can more easily narrow down the number of options to be investigated further during a diagnosis. This, in turn, will lessen the pension burden of the working population because doctors will spend more years working and generating tax revenues rather than studying (*Key Idea # 4* again).

Key attitudes and behaviors to remember from Step 2:

- Farting is good for you and the people around you, who either get exercise while running for shelter or inhale healthy gases
- Farting benefits society in many ways, notably by eliminating symptoms that may confuse physicians
- Farting should be mandatory

Actions and feelings log for Step 2:

	Freedom to fart	Feedback loop 1	Feedback loop 2	Feedback loop 3 etc.
Feel				
Act (underlined)		*SAMPLE – DO NOT WRITE HERE*		
Reflect				
Transcend				

Progress tracker for Step 2:

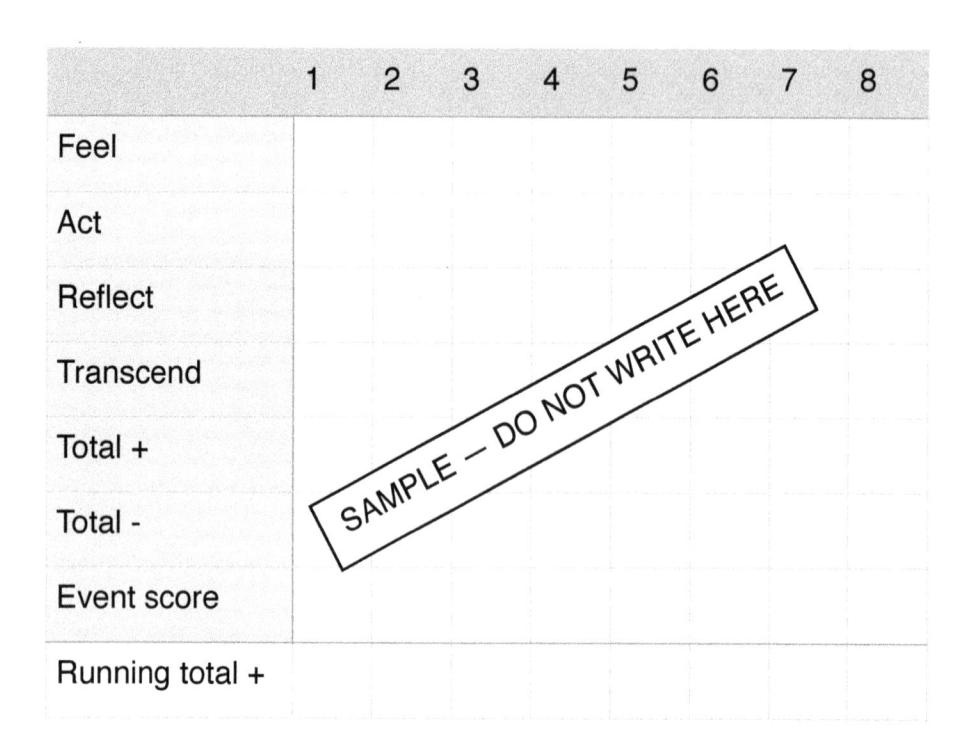

	1	2	3	4	5	6	7	8
Feel								
Act								
Reflect								
Transcend			*SAMPLE – DO NOT WRITE HERE*					
Total +								
Total -								
Event score								
Running total +								

~ 64 ~

6.
Step 3: Look to Man's Best Friend

"Besides love and sympathy, animals exhibit other qualities connected with the social instincts which in us would be called moral."—Chuck Darnwind

Even if human-canine relationship is thought to be the world's oldest human-animal liaison and most dogs are seen as members of the family rather than pets, canine abuse is still common. Abuse can be physical or psychological, and sometimes the latter can be far worse than the former because it ruins friendships, decimates self-esteem and often leaves victims without credibility because there are no visible traces. A fellow author went as far as to "blame it on the dog" in his book about farting. I immediately found the title repulsive and refused to even browse through it for inspiration, let alone buy it and read it. How dare he! Blame it on your best friend? And one that can't speak up for himself! Well, there are psychopaths everywhere, so I shouldn't be surprised. I hope he gets all his shoes chewed up and his garden dug up every day for the rest of his life.

Your dog *is* your best friend, and it is without doubt mutual. In case you haven't noticed, dogs fart without trying to stop it, not even when around friends. They don't wait for loud music on television or a truck to drive by and hope their fart will go unnoticed. They don't think that if they sit uncomfortably for a few minutes, cross their legs and squeeze their buttocks together, the fart will somehow be absorbed back into their intestines, and— voilà! —problem solved. The reason is simple: they don't consider farting a problem, but a natural bodily function that should not be obstructed. They simply wouldn't contemplate wasting energy on such an utterly futile undertaking. In a worst-case scenario, they would focus too much on controlling the fart and lose track of where they have buried all their bones, get frustrated and tear up another sofa cushion to let off steam. So they fart, without giving it any thought, much like dogs and humans bat their eyelids. They know that trying to stop a fart is as useless as trying to make cows belch into a handkerchief in an effort to reduce greenhouse gas emissions produced while they digest feed. Dogs don't understand if you yell at them for farting. They will look as sorry as a bloodhound who had all his bones stolen by the Great Dane next door if they get caught tearing a sofa cushion to shreds or chew your best shoes up until you can pass them off as sandals but have no clue what they have done wrong if you punish them for farting. They will think you have lost it. "I was lying here doing nothing, absolutely nothing, and now he's angry with me. Dooog, I need to re-activate my account on www.newmasterfinder.dog ASAP. Where did I bury my passwoof, again?"

I am sure you have noticed that when dogs play, it can come across as pretty rowdy. They chase each other, bite, wrestle, growl and bark. What are they arguing about, if in fact they are arguing? Maybe they are just trying to get a few essential points across. We too raise our voice if we believe our message or idea is worth repeating or accentuating, so that nobody misses the point, especially if we think we are right. Now, I cannot claim to be any kind of expert on dogs, but I have—like many of us—picked up a book or two on canine behavior and how to raise a dog. There are literally hundreds of books out there, and even though I may not have read a representative selection, I will simply ask the reader if you have ever come across a theory stating that dogs fight over farting? Do they ever attack one another because one dog farted and blamed one of the other dogs? I didn't think so. The fact is that dogs have 50 times the number of what are called olfactory receptors in their noses, which translates into a sense of smell which is at least 10,000 as acute as ours, and they still don't react! Think about the worst fart you ever smelled—your own or someone else's—and multiply that by 10,000! I guarantee you that you would empty your bowels in seconds flat, and it would still be unpleasant. And dogs don't even raise their eyebrows if they smell a fart. Clearly, one of the most intelligent species on Earth, with the most acute sense of smell among mammals, completely ignores farting or at least does not consider in sufficiently unpleasant to reprimand the perpetrator. How is that for evidence that farting is essentially a biological necessity and under no circumstances a source of disagreement or discomfort?

So, your best friend undoubtedly thinks you can fart around your best friend, whatever their species. It's also pretty clear that your best friend thinks you can fart with him lying at your feet. We also tend to refer to our fiancés and spouses as our best friends. By extension, you can fart in the presence of your wife, and by further extension your in-laws. Whether you like it or not, you also married them, so you can consider them your best friends. And, yes, best friends argue, so you simply have to accept the idea that your in-laws are on par with your dog friendship-wise. Once you are allowed to do something in the presence of your in-laws, it's settled: it's allowed anywhere, and in anybody's presence—

even if it does take courage and practice to fart around other people (cf. subsequent steps). Dogs are intelligent, caring and social beings, like us. They know.

If in doubt whether you should fart, ask yourself, "Would a dog fart here?"
(Key Idea # 5)

Walking the Dog

Have you noticed how people who walk their dog in a park easily connect and socialize, and you as a dogless person (if you don't have a dog) envy them as you take your Sunday stroll and look for somewhere to sit down and read yesterday's news again or listen to your "workout" playlist for the umpteenth time that week? You think, "How nice it would be to have a dog and chat with one of those friendly-looking persons…" Yes, dog owners connect easily, and they connect even more easily if:

- They have dogs of the same breed

- The dogs want to breed

- The dogs look like the owners. This is considered particularly charming

- The owners and the dogs behave in the same way. This reinforces the point above

It's that last point where farting comes in. We know that dogs consider farting as natural behavior, so they will fart in the park, and other dog owners will notice. In addition to making short replies such as "Yes", "No" and "Who, me?" sound like your dog's barks, you should also fart whenever the urge presents itself. This is particularly effective if the farts smell the same, which means you need to eat the same food as the dog. You have two basic choices:

- Serve the dog the same food as you eat

- Eat dog food

If you find dog food less appealing and the dog doesn't like sushi, pizza or mac and cheese, you have an issue and need to look for an alternative solution.

- Grind dog food in a blender and use as a condiment on your own food

- Replace ground beef with gradually increasing amounts of dog food

Basically, do whatever it takes to capitalize fully on the behavior replication effect, which helps us even more as scientific research proves that it reinforces itself over time. Dog owners and dogs looking and acting the same is the epitome of charm, and more so if you behave like twins in all respects.

"What about panting and drooling?" I hear you ask. "Do I need to do that if my dog does?" Don't worry, you already pant and drool mentally as you approach attractive specimens of your preferred gender, and they notice immediately—especially women. I also believe that actual panting and drooling helps, too, albeit with few incidents to prove my theory.

Top it all with farting with the same smell, and you are on your way out of single life—guaranteed.

Farting can help you find a suitable partner to procreate with
(Key Idea # 6)

Finally, any tree is the right tree to fart up.

> **Key attitudes and behaviors to remember from Step 3:**
>
> - Dogs are intelligent and social beings that fart when needed. As their best friends, we should too
> - "Blaming it on the dog" is just mean
> - Looking, behaving and farting like your own dog is charming

Actions and feelings log for Step 3:

	Freedom to fart	Feedback loop 1	Feedback loop 2	Feedback loop 3 etc.
Feel				
Act (underlined)				
Reflect				
Transcend				

SAMPLE – DO NOT WRITE HERE

Progress tracker for Step 3:

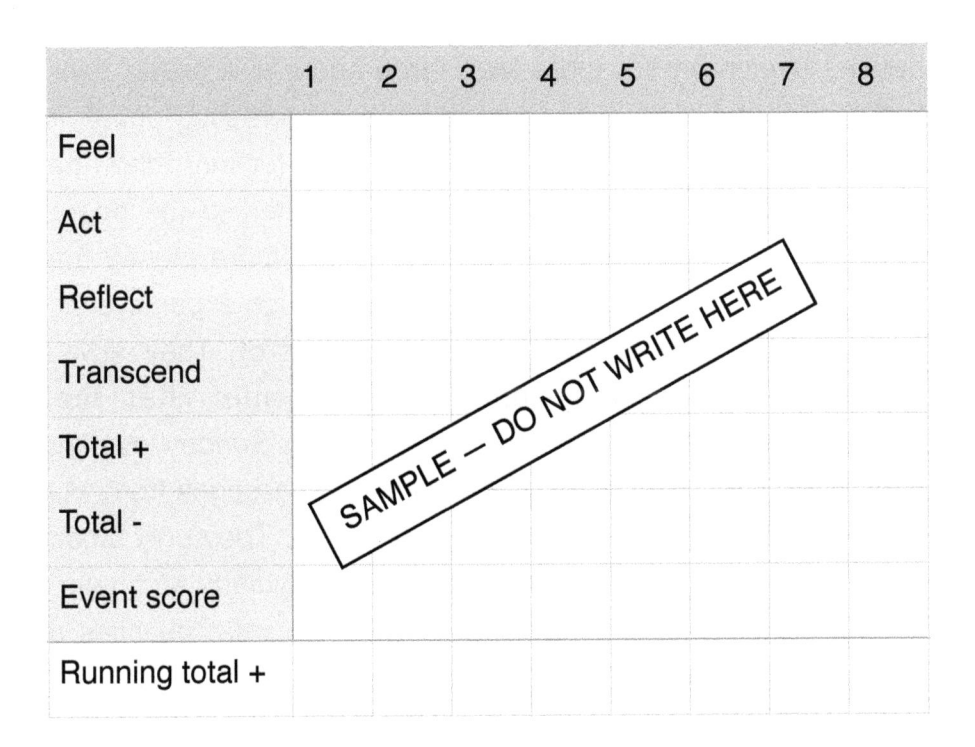

	1	2	3	4	5	6	7	8
Feel								
Act								
Reflect								
Transcend								
Total +								
Total -								
Event score								
Running total +								

SAMPLE – DO NOT WRITE HERE

7.
Step 4: Fart Around the Guys/Girls

"A friend is what the fart needs all of the time." —Henry van Dyke

You know the type. There's always one of the guys who wears the latest fashion brands without as much as a stain or a crease, smells of the most fashionable cologne, polishes his shoes every day even if they haven't been worn for more than three hours to a ballet, drinks like a bird, and always has another, more interesting option for the evening. "Sorry I can't be with you guys for more than half an hour, because I promised I'd take Gretchen to the opera." These guys always have parents who make more money than yours, they drive a Porsche or a Ferrari, and use expensive skin care products that women notice the effect of. They always cough into a monogrammed handkerchief that their housekeeper ironed a batch of fifteen of on Sunday evening, they never spill wine, and they can cite long passages from "*A la recherche du temps perdu*" by Marcel Proust. They only smoke expensive cigars, if at all. They play tennis regularly and have a low handicap in golf. (I, for one, don't know what qualifies as low, which is why I didn't say 12 or 6, or whatever "low" is.) They watch football and other team sports but are not anywhere near as passionate about their teams as the rest of us. We often wonder if they have a favorite team. If they claim they have one, they are incapable of quoting any statistics or discussing a player's strengths and weaknesses.

In short, they are everything the rest of us wanted to be but failed to become—with the exception of the unenthusiastic attitude towards team sports. To be fair to them, they spend a lot of energy managing pressure from mothers, grandmothers, great aunts and eligible bachelorettes from the same neighborhood, unless they already married one, of course. They would genuinely like to be in two camps full-time but find themselves torn between them and risk pleasing nobody, particularly Gretchen. Men being men, they gravitate towards the easy way out, but at a cost.

Because of all these traits and borderline effeminate behavior, they are not one of the guys. We accept their presence and would welcome them as full-fledged members rather than hang-arounds if they would give up at least a few of those annoying habits. They don't have to sell their Porsche or give up dating Gretchen. She is of course attractive but slightly arrogant, the way she glances haughtily into our man caves, expecting us to pick up the empty beer cans from the floor just because she showed up to tow him back into civilization.

Actually, none of those habits alone or in any combination with one another disqualifies a man from being one of the guys. We all come from different backgrounds, have diverse cultural interests (as long as there is a ball of a certain dimension involved), and dream of dating snotty, rich women. And deep down, we don't mind being guided firmly by our girlfriends or spouses. Sometimes they know better, and we don't realize until later.

The real problem with these men is that they never fart in the presence of another person, least of all a woman. What does such a man fear? That the man cave will smell even worse? That he will be disinherited? That Gretchen will break up with him and go back to Carlton? That his Hermès underwear will be ruined and the housekeeper will think less of him or—worse—tell his mother?

Real men don't think like that. You don't have to shower twice a year and live in a cave or semi-permanently in a man cave to be a real man, but you don't let other people's reaction to perfectly normal human behavior guide you in the choices you make in life. Real men go and have fun with the guys when they feel the need for it AND it suits the rest of the family, i.e. if the dog feels confident that the family members left in the house are capable of feeding him. Being a real man has nothing to do with ignoring the needs of those near and dear. In fact, quite the opposite—real men do everything required to feed and protect their families, including exercising their civil rights to listen to the signals their bodies send.

Also, friends should support each other in their current or budding relationships. If one of the guys or girls has an attractive partner in sight, we tend to encourage him or her to make the next decisive move, guide their behavior and give unsolicited advice. Very often, one piece of advice is to be yourself, right? Part of being yourself is to fart when the need arises. Charity begins at home, so it would be hypocritical to suggest that a friend should be himself in a relationship and not accept that he farts in your presence.

If you want to be one of the guys, you must be a real man. Real men don't give a toss if Gretchen's snotty nose is filled with sulfuric compounds for a few disagreeable seconds. Real men do excuse themselves when they fart, knowing it may be unpleasant. But they never try to hide the fact that they are men with basic physical needs. After all, other kinds of physical needs are sometimes discussed in great detail when men meet. Not farting in such a setting would be the epitome of hypocrisy. Simply put, if you are one of the guys, you fart. If you don't, questions will be asked. Nasty questions. Not about your sexual orientation—you are still one of the guys if you are gay. I'm talking questions about your integrity, your respect for the course of nature, and your attitude to personal freedom. Fart, and avoid these questions. Be one of the guys.

Key attitudes and behaviors to remember from Step 4:

- Not farting around the guys/girls is pure hypocrisy
- You'll never be one of the guys if you don't fart

Actions and feelings log for Step 4:

	Freedom to fart	Feedback loop 1	Feedback loop 2	Feedback loop 3 etc.
Feel				
Act (underlined)		*SAMPLE – DO NOT WRITE HERE*		
Reflect				
Transcend				

Progress tracker for Step 4:

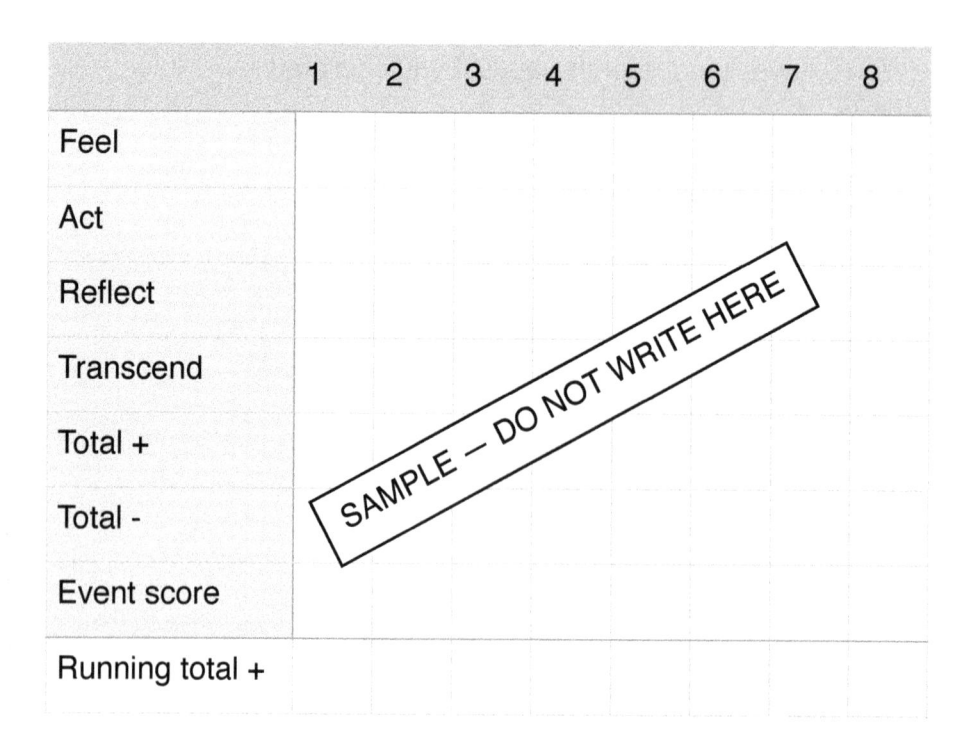

	1	2	3	4	5	6	7	8
Feel								
Act								
Reflect								
Transcend				*SAMPLE – DO NOT WRITE HERE*				
Total +								
Total -								
Event score								
Running total +								

8.
Step 5: Fart in the Presence of Your Partner

"We don't judge the people we love."—Jean-Paul Fartre

Most of us who don't have a dog consider our partner or spouse our best friend. One should think that taking the step from farting around your best friend to farting while being with your wife or husband, is a fairly easy step to take. Yes and no. Some of the moments that we share with our partners are, on the face of it, similar to the most precious moments with our high school or college chums. To an extent, this is true. There are, however, a few additional challenges when graduating to the fart-with-your-partner level.

For one, you have sex.

Also, you tend to be naked more often with your partner than with your best friends, at least where I grew up. You are in the shower together, and you get dressed in the bedroom together. Is farting natural in these situations? This far into the book, you should answer that question yourself with a resounding "Yes!" Why is it natural? Because it always is! You don't have to make it more complicated than that. Whatever you do, don't even think about saying something like this:

- "Uhm, honey, sorry I farted, it's just that I thought when we are naked, we are sort of like, uhm cave dwellers, and then... uhm... less civilized, I mean, we're as civilized as we always are, I mean we're back to nature, in a way. Except I mean it's not like we're not going to use the toilet or anything like that. You know what I mean!"

- "No, I don't! What do you mean? Am I actually hearing you say that, just because we are naked, we can fart like savages? Are you going to hit me on the head with a club and pull me into your cave by my hair? Is that what's going to happen next?"

This is a discussion you can't win, so, again, keep it simple. Just say, "It's natural." (And by now you should have no inclination whatsoever to blame it on the dog lying quietly in the corner.) Is there a risk of a temporary turn-off and no action taking place that evening? Yes, I am afraid so. A free human being will simply accept it as a fact of life and move on.

Next, you have in-laws.

If you manage to behave exactly as you please around your in-laws, you have cracked the code and should write a book. It'll be a best-seller, guaranteed. Now, most people take a quick look at the toilet seat when the in-laws are expected, they fold the empty pizza boxes half-heartedly and do their best to stuff them down an almost full garbage bin. They empty ashtrays if they in fact dare to smoke when in-laws are visiting, and they don't put their feet on the table. As to farting, it is simply out of the question. You could get away with wearing a stained wife-beater shirt or swatting a fly with your open hand without washing it afterwards. You can even get away with crushing a beer can on your forehead and the odd sexist joke late in the evening, after a few drinks. But you are destined for doom and gloom in the People's Republic of Inlawia if you fart. We're talking serious human rights violations here, far beyond sleep deprivation, solitary confinement and summary judgments. In fact, many of us would prefer an extra-judicial execution to put us out of our misery, should we be caught farting in the presence of our in-laws. Whatever you do, do not try to bribe your way out of the situation. It will only worsen your predicament, if anything—especially if you persuade children to take the blame in exchange for a cookie or an ice cream. The President and the First Gentleman will get personally involved in your case and make sure your spouse will be disinherited, you will lose access to the family cabin with immediate effect, you will receive scornful glances that pierce your body like radioactive needles in a voodoo doll until your last day on Earth, and you should not be surprised if a couple of child protection agents show up at your front door the day after. You may as well start preparing your defense the very second the gas reaches your mother-in-law's nostrils. Is it child abuse to fart with your children in the room? Of course not, but be prepared to explain why you are a good parent and are giving them a safe upbringing in a harmonious home with lots of love and affection. To be prepared for this situation and provide evidence that you are not harming your children in any way, shape or form, it is wise to record a few video footages of everyday situations where you are all dressed nicely, the house is clean, you have prepared a good home-made meal, you spend quality time at the dinner table, and round off the evening with an edifying game in all congeniality. It doesn't have to be anything lavish, or a holiday such as Christmas dinner. The child protection agents will see through such an episode and discard it as constructed evidence, and so will the court. Keep multiple copies of the footage, just in case.

Why should you fart in the presence of your in-laws if you risk being branded as the black sheep of the family and disinherited? To answer that question, we will rely on neuro-scientific research, which shows that our brains consume more energy when we perform tasks we don't master or prefer to avoid. This explains why we are exhausted after having our in-laws over for Sunday lunch, while having a few friends over for home-made pizza makes us feel relaxed and ready to start a new work week full of energy. The amount of physical work is roughly the same, but our brains are pushed to the limit because we spend energy to conceal who we are. Most of us are poor liars, even worse actors, and like to avoid pretending for extended periods of time.

To save yourself from these recurring fatiguing ordeals, you need to be true to yourself and simply stop the charade. Who are you? Like most of us, first and foremost a farter. The easy way to start being yourself around your in-laws is to start farting freely, and take it from there. Soon you will start saying what you think, and stop pretending you agree with what everybody around the table says. Shin guards are recommended in an interim period, when your significant other will voice his or her concern through non-verbal communication under the table. Believe me—it's worth the pain and the late-night de-briefing sessions in the master bedroom. At the end of the day, you need to ask yourself if you want to show up at work exhausted every other Monday and jeopardize your career, or be yourself and gain mentally and professionally.

Then you have romantic outings, such as wedding anniversary dinners, the odd movie date, and maybe a one-on-one in a skating rink.

In all these situations, you aim to have fun, spend quality time together, or relive great moments from the past. The thing is that humans subconsciously want to display their achievements: their career, their smart and healthy children, their Tesla, their house, their luxury holidays, and so on. And trophy wives or husbands. The trophies are just as perfect as the other objects of desire, simply flawless (that's how love works). Perfect life companions are well-read, well-behaved and generally attractive. If they cough, they excuse themselves and do their best to avoid coughing into the air. If you fart, you embarrass your date, and your value as a trophy drops like a dot-com share at the turn of the century (for the millennials reading this book, search for "dot-com bubble" on the internet). You can forget about current investors thinking longer term and piling up on those cheap shares. It's Black Monday for all your personal assets: your looks, your witty remarks, the way you dress, and—clearly—the way you smell. The question is: should you care? If you genuinely love the person you are with, you will care as a reflex. But, again, should you? If your partner cares as much as you for him or her, he or she will not interpret a single fart as an indication that you intend to make life miserable for him or her. On the contrary, you signal many other, positive things that far outweigh the transient discomfort of inhaling someone's intestinal gases. Refer to the ten statements you make by farting freely, and read Step 6 carefully, particularly the section explaining why farting in front of a mortgage officer is a good idea.

Finally, remember the point about two of the gases farts contain are flammable? If I were to guess, the words "stop farting" are uttered more frequently between couples than in any other setting. Now, this is a paradox. You love each other, and you tell each other to keep accumulating flammable gases in your bowels? Not only that, but trying to retain gases inside you has many other adverse effects. We can therefore infer that a conversation (wife-to-husband monolog) that goes like this:

Him: (FART)

Her: Stop farting in the living room! I'm sick of telling you!

...means this:

Him: (FART)

Her: For heaven's sake, I have told you many times to keep building up flammable gases in your bowels. When will you listen and actually do it? I don't care if you explode, get heartburn or indigestion, or damage your colon or get arthritis. You hardly ever move anyway! And stop eating healthy fibers, while you're at it. I'm serious. And don't even think about exploding on the new couch. This is the final warning! Stop farting or you are no longer welcome in this house!

Love works in mysterious ways.

If you truly love your partner, you should share your newly acquired knowledge about the financial, spiritual and health benefits of farting freely, and you can both live long, happy and healthy lives together. It's what you promised each other in the first place, so what took you so long? Isn't this book a life saver, and now also a relationship saver? Remember, new relationships, not to mention divorce, cost money, so, again, farting benefits you financially (*Key Idea # 4*).

> **Key attitudes and behaviors to remember from Step 5:**
>
> - If you love your partner, fart in his or her presence
> - Your brain prefers that you fart around your in-laws
> - Partners who tell each other to stop farting actually dislike each other, as they want each other to risk that their bowels explode

Actions and feelings log for Step 5:

	Freedom to fart	Feedback loop 1	Feedback loop 2	Feedback loop 3 etc.
Feel				
Act (underlined)				
Reflect				
Transcend				

SAMPLE – DO NOT WRITE HERE

Progress tracker for Step 5:

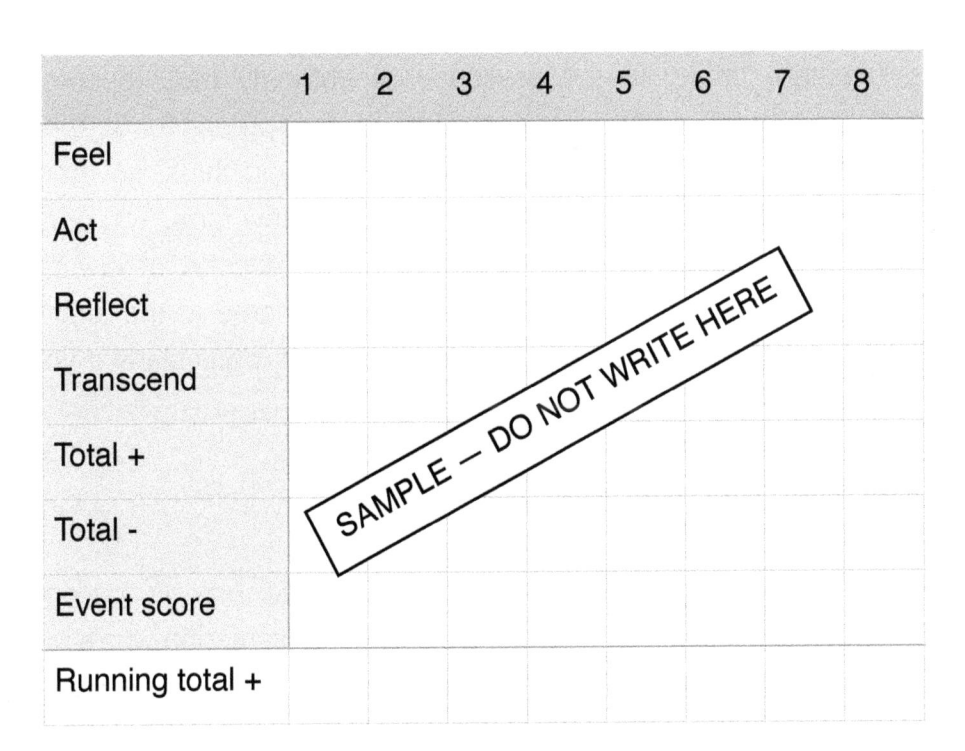

	1	2	3	4	5	6	7	8
Feel								
Act								
Reflect								
Transcend								
Total +								
Total -								
Event score								
Running total +								

SAMPLE – DO NOT WRITE HERE

9.
Step 6: Fart in the Presence of Authority

"To fart is human, to forbid derisory."—Alexander Poof

This is the second-to-last and most challenging step, and probably the one that will take the longest. As with the other steps, doing it once is insufficient. In order to liberate yourself completely and become a truly free man or woman, farting in the presence of authority must become second nature, much like dogs fart in the presence of their master. You face authority more often than you think, so there should be numerous occasions to try the first few farts. You don't have to wait until the next time you are in a court of law for whatever reason and fart when stating your name to the judge, although it would have been an excellent start, particularly if you are a defendant.

The Parking Attendant

An authority most people don't think of as one is parking attendants. We just see them as a pain and as someone who's out to make your life miserable for no good reason. Few people would disagree with this statement. But they are also an authority—albeit in a narrowly defined area, and one that you should respect, even if your first thought when seeing an attendant put a ticket on your windshield is to throw whatever you have in your hands at him or her. "Hey, dip*%&$, get a life!" or "Are you serious? I was just picking up my kid, and didn't park for more than three minutes, you worthless piece of %#+!" are frequently uttered phrases on the streets of congested cities these days.

As I'm sure you have experienced, talking your way out of it is completely futile. It's like arguing with the referee at a soccer game. They never budge, and never will. My advice is that it's better to use the occasion as part of a journey to become a Free Human Being rather than to argue with a CSI (certified stubborn individual) in order to save, say, 20$. It just won't happen.

What do you do? Keep calm and walk slowly towards your car, not taking any shortcuts or jaywalking. There is no point rushing, as you have now effectively paid for parking, and you don't want to break sweat with little to show for it or risk getting hit by a car while running across the street, not noticing the car with a madman at the wheel—a frothing looney who has just got his second parking ticket that day.

Use the occasion to learn how to avoid parking tickets in the future and ask the attendant to explain exactly where you went wrong. As soon as you feel a fart coming, let it go. You are a human being, and you are free. Bear in mind that you should not fart in such a way that you show disrespect or contempt for the attendant or his work by saying e.g. "Let me tell you, you little (fart sound)." After all, he's just doing his job, which is important for an orderly traffic situation in cities. Simply fart when it feels right for you. That's what freedom is about (*Key Idea # 7* below).

Once you feel comfortable farting during an every-day encounter such as a lessons-learned session with a parking attendant, you are ready to take it to the next level.

The Bouncer

Let's consider bouncers for a while. Generally well-built men who are ready to take decisive action when required, they are—like parking attendants—not what you generally think of as authority, although they most certainly exercise authority with immediate consequences for those affected. I assume most readers are not the kind of people to be expelled from bars because of rude behavior on a regular basis, but it can and does happen to the best of us. I, for one, have several friends who have been refused entry to night clubs because they had had a little too much to drink. In short, they were visibly intoxicated and would have been better off getting some sleep. Regardless whether you are at risk of being turned away when standing in line outside a popular night spot, it's the right occasion to practice and further develop your free behavior by farting exactly when and if the need arises. Again, you do not want to provoke authority by farting when they act contrary to your expectations. It is bound to make matters worse, if anything. Don't force freedom upon yourself—live it when the urge comes.

> **Freedom is natural, never forced**
> **(Key Idea # 7)**

Whether you are talking to friends, having a casual discussion with the bouncer, or simply standing there waiting patiently to get inside and drink from the horn of plenty, any time is a good time to fart. That said, in your quest to become a Free Farter, it's accepted to time the fart so that Authority becomes aware that you are there and you are free. There is, of course, a risk that farting will be interpreted as a sign of rogue behavior inside the establishment, and you will be asked to leave the premises. That should not bother a Truly Free Person or anyone who aspires to become one. The long-term benefits simply outweigh the temporary loss of access to the transient pleasures one may indulge in after midnight. On the road to Absolute Freedom, you must be prepared to make some sacrifices, such as not having that last couple of craft beers or frozen margaritas with your friends. I know it hurts, but once you have come this far, there is no turning back. Accept losing a battle on one front, when winning the war is what matters.

Given that some bouncers may come across as intimidating, farting freely in their presence is quite an achievement, but you are not there yet. Time to move up the ladder and get one step closer to shedding the shackles.

The Loan Officer

In contrast to the parking attendant or the bouncer, a loan officer is an authority whose decisions may have a long-term effect on your daily life. Most people would try their best to behave as civilized as possible when exposing their personal finances with the aim to place a bid on the dream house or the sports car you always wanted. And most people mistakenly consider not farting as civilized behavior. In fact, it's probably on top of the list of don'ts valid for all sorts of serious meetings with authorities. You may sneeze, cough, smoke if allowed, clear your throat, wipe sweat off your hand onto your pants, answer mobile phone calls and do all sorts of impolite things. But whatever you do, don't fart. Your fly can be open—it's an honest mistake. Your bra strap can show—it's perfectly acceptable to be in a hurry, but don't fart! That's the prevailing attitude, and it's simply wrong.

Truly Free People make more money than the average simply because they are more innovative due to their free spirit, and have the guts to think and act differently. They are promoted more frequently and are more likely to be successful entrepreneurs. Truly Free People also have better health than average and will consequently earn higher lifetime salaries than average due to a longer working life, so any mortgage officer or other credit officer worth his salt will appreciate that even if you don't make more money than the national average when you apply for credit, your prospects as a Truly Free Person are far superior to those who always follow the rules and never think outside the box. In the age of the robots, creativity is at a premium, and free-spirited people are clearly more creative than others. Consequently, by farting, you get across that you have a higher earnings potential than others and will be more likely to get the mortgage you need to buy the dream home. (*Key Idea # 4 again*—Farting may help you financially.)

When talking to the mortgage officer—and any other authority, for that matter—do not try to be funny. It's tempting for an aspiring Truly Free Person to make a joke out of farting and say things like, "I can always place a stink bid" and then fart when discussing a prospective home purchase that appears to be outside your range. Mortgages are serious business, especially in today's volatile world economy. You want to come across as a free-spirited person who challenges the established, not a jester. Whether the likes of Steve Jobs and other creative people fart as freely as they want to, is not entirely clear, but it is beyond doubt that they cherished the freedom they had. Few of us will end up in the same league, but we should all the same share their core values, freedom in particular. By farting freely in the presence of authority, we convey that we have a free body and soul, and may well be destined for greatness, albeit at a more modest level than the late Mr. Jobs et al.

The Judge

Not many of us have stood before a judge as a defendant, at least not in a criminal court. For those of us who have, it's been about misdemeanors, a dispute with your landlord, or filing for custody in case of a divorce. Also, more often than not, these cases don't end up as trials as such, but as settlements outside the courtroom. Nevertheless, you do have to explain your acts or position to the judge, and the situation will come across as intimidating for many of us.

In many court cases, timing is a crucial element in your courtroom strategy, and one that you are wise to deliberate and rehearse multiple times with your lawyer. The closing statement is generally considered the most important step in a case, and literally where you win or lose the case, based on how convincing your lawyer is, how he or she argues for or against the relevance and quality of evidence presented, and how he or she counters arguments presented by the opposition. Choice of words, tone of voice, and body language matter, too. And if you are in a position to save your best line of reasoning for the closing statement, and the best arguments for why the opposition has a weak case, you are most certainly one step closer to winning the case.

By now, I have probably led you to believe that there is an optimal timing for farting in the courtroom, or that you shouldn't fart at all, because of the solemnity emanating from every corner of the room, with your nation's flag or coat of arms in a prominent position.

Nothing could be further from the truth. There is no right or wrong time to fart in a courtroom. You can fart at any time: when sitting next to your counsel, when approaching the bench if you are a lawyer, in the witness stand, or when the judge reads the ruling. Any time. Trust me. Why would you trust me when so much can be at stake, including life imprisonment? Remember the statements you make by farting freely?

"I am honest."

"I am free."

"I want all people to be free."

Surely, these are statements that will ring well in any state with the rule of law as the mainstay of society.

That said, there is a catch: the judge has a lot of leeway when it comes to determining what he or she considers contemptuous behavior, which may be any kind of disrespectful behavior or any act that is contrary to the dignity of the courtroom. How can you safeguard yourself against the risk of getting a fine—or worst case—a jail sentence just because you fart in the wrong moment? The answer to this apparent dilemma is found in *Key Idea # 7: Freedom is natural, never forced.* This simply means that you should not show blatant disrespect by saying things like, "Do you want to know what I think of this sentence?" and then fart. You will for sure be held in contempt and face the consequences.

As a Truly Free Person, you cherish freedom and respect people and institutions alike. There is no contradiction here—you can do both, simply by behaving naturally, listening to your body, and separating basic body functions and the human communication process. You wouldn't bring a pinch of ground pepper to the courtroom, sniff it in the right moment and sneeze in the face of the judge, would you? Should you fart audibly and be reprimanded on the spot, you may not have the opportunity to defend yourself there and then, but—in case you do get the opportunity—your defense should go along these lines, depending on why you are in court:

"Your Honor, the constitution of our great nation states that I'm innocent until proven guilty, so I consider myself a free man. If I am free, so is the gas inside me. I therefore respectfully reserve the right to expel gas to maintain the physiological balance inside me, Your Honor."

Should you end up in this apparently awkward situation, with a risk of being sentenced to an additional jail term, it is an excellent opportunity to promote civil liberties by appealing to the judge's willingness to make an historic ruling. Judges are ambitious and well-educated people with—it goes without saying—a keen sense of justice. This doesn't mean that they will necessarily accept your proposal, but—if well-formulated and prepared—it will most certainly be possible to persuade a judge in a good mood to make a ruling for uninhibited farting in their courtroom. If your proposal goes along these lines, ideally handed over on a piece of paper or a USB thumb drive for the judge's convenience, you will not only change your own standing for the better—you will also contribute to improving human rights nation or state-wide:

(COURT NAME)
IN RE (COURT CASE).

ORDER FOR ALLOWING FLATUS EXPULSION DURING COURT PROCEEDINGS

WHEREAS, the Constitution of (name of your state or country) stipulates that every man is born free;

WHEREAS, a defendant may be detained in custody for the duration of the court proceedings, such detention only deprives the defendant of those liberties that are necessary to restrict in order to safeguard the completion of a fair trial;

WHEREAS, every human produces and regularly disposes of intestinal gas as part of the digestion process;

WHEREAS, the waste substances, including intestinal gases, contained inside a human body remain legally and physically inseparable from the body itself;

WHEREAS, the act of suppressing natural bodily functions may reasonably lead to loss of concentration or focus on the matter of inquiry, whether inside or outside a court of law;

WHEREAS, the excretion of bodily fluids poses a threat to public health due to risk of contagion and requires immediate action to remove such excretions from the courtroom;

WHEREAS, expelling gas poses no such threat nor inconvenience; and,

WHEREAS, it is an observable fact that a significant proportion of all acts of expelling intestinal gas are strictly or partly involuntary;

NOW, THEREFORE, IT IS HEREBY ORDERED AND ADJUDGED AS FOLLOWS:

The act of expelling intestinal gases in a court of law can be held in contempt of court under the sole condition that an audible flatus expulsion is willfully released at such time as to replace a single term or expression in a sentence in the English language —or another language spoken during the court proceedings and translated by an interpreter authorized by the court—, thereby conveying a disrespectful message or opinion to any member of the court;

Under all other circumstances, the act of expelling intestinal gases during, before or after court proceedings, is condoned unconditionally;

The repeated act of suppressing flatus expulsion during court proceedings, as evidenced by frequent visits to sanitary facilities, visible physical uneasiness, or requests to repeat statements made by other members of the court, will in and of itself qualify as contemptuous behavior.

LET JUDGMENT BE ENTERED Accordingly.

(Date, signature, and court)

The Priest at Your Wedding Ceremony

Not all authorities are out to make life miserable for you. In fact, many of them are public servants who get a pay check every month because we pay our taxes and expect value for money in return, or at least a tax return that doesn't make you cry. In some countries, the priest is one such public servant. And in countries where he is not a public servant, you generally tend to finance him or her anyway, through donations to the church. Either way, he or she should treat you as a customer rather than a parish member he or she can patronize, regardless of whether he or she has a direct line to a divine being and can influence the general environment and quality of your afterlife quite dramatically.

Of course, not every encounter with your local priest or shaman is about whether you or your recently deceased relative will get stuck with Jack the Ripper or Mother Theresa at the dinner table for all eternity—there are a few happy occasions too.

Your Big Day is finally there. You and your spouse-to-be want the occasion to be perfect, with all old, new and blue items devoid of even the most minute imperfection. You brush your teeth and your tongue for ten minutes rather than the regular three, suck mints all the way to the church, and move like a sloth to make sure you don't break a single drop of sweat until well after the ceremony. You clear your throat continually and practice stating the clearest, most heartfelt and most sincere "I do" ever recorded—one that immediately brings tears into your parents' and prospective in-laws' eyes, and makes warm glances cross the aisle as if to unite the two families through an unbreakable bond made in Heaven (or however many are involved these days. Sometimes the priest has to work with fractions and address "the 3 and 2/7 families about to be united in holy matrimony").

Those who subscribe to conventional wisdom and traditional social etiquette would consider farting the absolute last thing you want to do at anybody's wedding, especially your own, and definitely if you are a man. Should the bride fart, it could be attributed to understandable nervousness, or maybe because she is pregnant. The groom has no excuses whatsoever. But we know better.

Should you happen to fart during the ceremony, most people would expect the priest to look at you with a reproaching air as if to say, "I am seconds away from calling this ceremony off. This is unheard of. I make the rules here, and you just broke one of the top three." Whatever you do—and you will probably be taken by surprise yourself, especially if you say "I.." and then fart—don't look down, mumble something unintelligible to yourself, cough or excuse yourself to the priest. If there is a moment in life where you should speak the truth, it is now. And you should be yourself. You fart, I fart. We all fart. If you don't fart when everybody knows that we all fart, what else are you hiding? What else are you pretending? Is the planned marriage a front? If so, for what? In today's turbulent world with renewed political tension and internet fraud, you can't really trust anyone, especially those who suppress natural behaviors. I would turn it around: you **should** fart at your wedding to prove that you are sincere and truthful, meaning that your spouse will feel confident that your marriage won't be a succession of nasty revelations. And forget completely about the priest: you're his or her customer, and the customer is always right.

Because my advice defies conventional thinking quite dramatically, let me spell this one out more clearly:

It's a good idea to fart at your wedding ceremony because:

- You will come across as truthful

- You will be considered sincere

- You do not want to hide anything from your future spouse, especially on your big day. So you want to start right

- Natural behavior is expected from you from this day onwards. Courtship is over, no point in strutting like a wood grouse

The fact of the matter is that many couples—perhaps even all—fart more than they kiss. If they can't behave naturally when they promise each other to live together as husband and wife until death do them part, when can they?

Knowing what people who fart freely stand for, you would

probably agree with me that a better closing statement for the ceremony would be, "You may fart with the bride."

The Child Protection Agent

Now things are getting serious. I certainly hope you never see one on your doorstep. If you do, I hope it's because someone found that your habit of farting in the presence of children is a sign of child abuse. Remember the evidence I suggested that you collect? I mean, real evidence that you are a caring family man or woman? It may come in handy now, but let's assume that you are contacted as a potential witness of less-than-ideal parenting in your neighborhood. Either way, this is definitely a situation where you want to come across as truthful, and that you have nothing to hide. What do we know about farting now? It's probably the single most effective way to convey a clear message that everything you say is the truth, the whole truth and nothing but the truth. Imagine that one or two of them is on your doorstep, you are about to ask them to come in and have a seat, and you realize you need to fart and that it will be loud. Very loud. Many people will tell a white lie, saying something like, "Please wait, I just need to check how my little one is doing," and quickly sneak into the room closest to the front door, and then fart. The problem is that if they hear you, they know immediately exactly what you are: a liar. Needless to say, this would be a really bad start of a potentially grim process. The easy way to avoid it? You got it: fart freely. First impression is very important.

The Highway Patrol Officer

The highway patrol officer is quite possibly the most intimidating authority of them all, at least before you end up behind bars. A typical specimen is well-built, sports a short-sleeved shirt without displaying as much as the most minuscule goose bump even if the temperature is approaching freezing, and wears mirrored sunglasses where you only see a tiny, scared version of yourself, shaking like a leaf. It only makes his voice sound even deeper when he asks—or commands—you to step outside the car, and you immediately lose track of time and place, knowing that you will have problems explaining the course of events in any kind of congruent way, however innocent your actions may have been.

As mentioned in a few other situations above, this is not the time to be funny. Do not fall for the temptation to fart and say, "Guess I've had too many donuts today. Does it happen to you too, officer? I'll bet it does. Oh, and by the way, have you noticed what the donut hole looks like?"

You will no doubt end up in trouble if you do anything of the sort. Like the parking attendant, the highway patrol officer deserves respect—not just because he has the authority and means to make life miserable for you, but because he is doing his job.

As with other authorities, fart only when necessary.

In this scenario, however, your fart probably won't go unnoticed. Expect to hear a deep voice asking, "**Was that a fart that I heard, ma'am**? Are you trying to be **funny**? Are you trying to say something? I can assure you there's nothing funny about the situation you are in." Assuming you were pulled over for, say, speeding, your reply should be, "I'm a great believer in freedom, officer, and I respect your efforts to protect the public from criminals and reckless drivers. It is actually harmful to your health to suppress farting. Hence, if more people fart, there will be more money for law enforcement because we need to spend less money on healthcare."

Clearly, there is no guarantee that the above reasoning will be understood and accepted, so you need to have at least a couple of logically or emotionally appealing explanations for why you consider farting a human right, or natural behavior, or something that most people's health would benefit from. You can also refer to the law, but that can easily backfire and be interpreted as smart-ass behavior. This is exactly why I saved the highway patrol officer for last—you need to assess the situation and the officer's or officers' mood and reactions. Maybe a simple, "Yes, officer, I farted, but only because I had to," will suffice. If you want some time away from your family and employer and can't afford another vacation, you can crack the donut joke. That one is bound to generate a reaction. You will feel free-spirited when you utter those words, but at a cost.

Key attitudes and behaviors to remember from Step 6:

- You should fart in front of any authority, as it will benefit you in the long run
- If you want to fart on a parking attendant, do it, but casually
- Of all authorities that you should fart in front of, the priest at your wedding ceremony is the most important

Actions and feelings log for Step 6:

	Freedom to fart	Feedback loop 1	Feedback loop 2	Feedback loop 3 etc.
Feel				
Act (underlined)		*SAMPLE – DO NOT WRITE HERE*		
Reflect				
Transcend				

Progress tracker for Step 6:

	1	2	3	4	5	6	7	8
Feel								
Act								
Reflect								
Transcend				*SAMPLE – DO NOT WRITE HERE*				
Total +								
Total -								
Event score								
Running total +								

10.
Step 7: Look People in the Eyes When You Fart— And Enjoy It!

"Don't give up the ship in a storm because you cannot hold back the winds."—Thomas More

We all breathe the same air. As one math-savvy person calculated, we have on average 227 air molecules of any dead person's last breath in our lungs in any given moment. This will hold for any relative and any celebrity, including Jim Morrison's, John F. Kennedy's, Jack the Ripper's or Hitler's last breath.

The same person estimates that each time you inhale, approximately 4.7 trillion molecules that passed through the lungs of a carpenter's son who lived 2,000 years ago and was unpopular with the occupying Romans, find their way to your lungs.

Since a lot of the gases we fart are in fact swallowed air, it goes without saying that we also inhale air molecules that people farted into the air we all breathe. But how much? Let's do the math, using Marilyn Monroe as an example. (I chose an attractive female who died young, purely for diversity reasons.)

- Marilyn Monroe died at 36, while the carpenter's son died at 33, so our lungs probably contain 36/33 x 4.7 trillion = 5.1 trillion molecules that she exhaled in the course of her short but eventful life.

- According to one study (numerous studies probed into the matter), the average person farts 10 times a day for a total of 1 liter/U.S. quart of gases and breathes approximately 15,000 liters/U.S. quarts of air.

- That makes the ratio of farting to breathing volumes roughly 1:15,000 for the average person.

If we assume that the gases we fart are not absorbed by the surroundings in a vastly different way from the air we exhale, we constantly have 340 million molecules from Marilyn Monroe's farts in our lungs.

What does this tell us? That you can pretend that farting doesn't exist, that you and people in your entourage never fart, that only unpolished rogues fart, and so on, but you can't escape from the fact that we all produce—and inhale—the same gases as everyone else. I can guarantee you that every throne ever built, every leather-clad executive chair ever sat in, and every silk bed linen used by Genghis Khan or Queen Margaret of Denmark—they have all felt a little heat from someone's rear end. (Did I just break my euphemism rule here? Well, sue me then.)

By farting, you also signal that your bodily functions are working, apart from those people can observe more directly. From that perspective, farting is a bit like dancing. You show to prospective mating partners that you are physically fit and able to feed and protect the family, and that you are no mutant and will contribute positively to the family and tribe gene pools. Much like pheromones play a role in sexual attraction, I believe that farting plays a similar role, and that—contrary to popular belief—*farting can help you find a suitable partner to procreate with (Key Idea # 6)*.

We have all had them—the once-in-a-lifetime extremely long or extremely loud TNT farts that make babies cry, old ladies drop their dentures on the floor and sleeping dogs open one eye and check if there are any armed intruders in the room. Or the fart series that are synchronized with each step you take, like marching soldiers on their way to the battlefield to defend our freedom. Or even the singing farts that announce to the world that it's a sunny day and we should all rejoice and celebrate our freedom with appropriate fanfare.

Sadly, these unique, life-altering events sometimes occur without witnesses, and you are the sole person to enjoy them and be bemused by their light-hearted, playful tones meandering through the air like carefree butterflies searching haphazardly for the most colorful flowers with the sweetest nectar.

The point about farting is not the free entertainment, and the desire many people have to show off around family, friends and colleagues. Funny farts are very much a there-and-then thing—you're either there or you miss out. How many anecdotes about farting have you heard and laughed out loud? Not many.

Enjoying farting—in addition to the funny episodes—is about cherishing our freedom, behaving naturally, and farting in front of anyone without looking away or taking a casual step to the side. Contrary to popular belief, you are on your way to becoming a superhuman if you fart without inhibitions in virtually anyone's presence. Look them in the eyes, fart as much as needed there and then—nothing more, nothing less—while continuing the conversation or whatever activity as if nothing has happened.

Enjoy That Feeling of Superiority

Think about it next time you absolutely need to fart and there is no other way out. At this point, most readers will have understood that the notion of a "way out" when you have a physical urge is simply an outdated, goody-two-shoes, straitjacket way of thinking. The way out is... you know where. Anyway, think that you are better than other people at appreciating the freedom your ancestors or maybe even yourself have worked hard for. Think that we all breathe the same air and that there isn't a person on Earth who hasn't smelled other people's farts hundreds of times. Think that you are better at focusing on the things that matter in life. Think that you are not petty, condescending or judgmental, like some people are. Think that you are better than other people at recognizing that humans are part of the animal kingdom and should learn to live with it.

Think all or some of this the next time you fart in front of someone and look him or her in the eyes, and you will feel superior. You won't necessarily—and probably shouldn't—smile when you fart and in the immediate aftermath, but I can assure you that you will feel an inner glow and look forward to the next time you can fart in other people's company and re-live that feeling of superiority.

To be clear, you should not enjoy farting with other people around you because you want them to experience something unpleasant. What you should enjoy is:

- Your superior understanding of freedom

- Your superior understanding of farting as a necessary and beneficial bodily function

- Your contribution to extended civil liberties and improved public health

Face Evil and Fight It

You hear it all the time:

- "Stop farting! It smells like a dead skunk!"
- "Don't fart in the living room!"
- "I've told you so many times to go to the bathroom if you need to fart!"

On the face of it, people who tell you to stop farting only seek to avoid the smell and find the habit altogether disgusting. This may come as a surprise, but:

People who tell you to stop farting are EVIL
(Key Idea # 8)

They are evil because:

- They want you to feel pain

- They want you to explode

- They want you to harm your colon

- They want you to eat unhealthy food and die young

- Some of them even want you to eat nothing at all

- They want you to get cancer

"Wait!" you think. "My parents told me to stop farting when I was a kid. And my grandmother too! And now my spouse! Are all the people I love EVIL? Surely, that can't be!"

I hate to break it to you, but it may well be that you have been surrounded by evil people throughout your entire upbringing. Try to think back to your childhood. You remember happy occasions like the day you got your first bike, Christmas Eve at your grandparents', and holding your first puppy. Now think back to everyday occasions, such as walking to school, hoping you wouldn't be bullied by the meanest kid on the block. And you remember being yelled at by your parents, your wrestling coach or soccer parents who thought your performance was poor and cost the team the victory. You also worried a lot about how your grandparents would react if you happened to break something or —heaven forbid—fart. You remember fear, right? The reason: kids are smart, they realize that some people are out to get you because they are evil. There were—and still are—far more evil people around you than you like to think.

And what about the Irish nobility and merchant class who gradually replaced professional farters with *uilleann* pipers— literally "elbow pipers"—sending hundreds of family men into unemployment and squalor? Undoubtedly evil, wouldn't you agree? Fair enough, maybe some of them didn't know other people's asses from other people's elbows, but that's no excuse.

Now, some people believe in humanity and claim there are no evil people, only evil acts. People do all sorts of things in difficult situations, under the influence of alcohol, or as a result of a passing bout of rage. In such cases, I would tend to agree that it's the acts that are evil, and not the people committing them. But what about serial killers? Do they just happen to commit unspeakable acts due to a momentary lapse of reason? Only the most fervent defenders of human nature would claim that these people are not evil.

So, then, can we agree that evil people do exist? Good.

What about people who repeatedly tell you not to fart? Effectively, they tell you to get abdominal pain, to contract all sorts of serious diseases, and to live an unhealthy life and die young. If that's not evil, I don't know what is. Of course, with an aging population and close to zero returns on our pension funds, dying young may prove to be a favorable outcome, but the evil people should not under any circumstances get credit for solving a massive financial issue for society and individuals alike.

The observant reader will think back to the universal human classification framework, according to which a negative attitude to free farting may be attributed to ignorance. This is of course correct but does not mean that there are inconsistencies in my reasoning, as the ignorant opponents of free farting are *Ignorant Wannabe* **Dictators**. Do you remember many benevolent dictators from your history classes? I didn't think so. Also, to stay alert and ready to defend yourself, you should consider all people who object to free farting as evil people. Whether there are one or two camps out there—the evil and the ignorant, or just the evil—doesn't matter that much. The important point here is that the minority you and I represent (assuming you are a devout Free Farter by now), needs to spread the word about the benefits of farting freely. By converting as many ignorant and evil people as possible to our creed, we are doing humanity a great favor. Which tools do we have at our disposal to deliver the Greater Good? As always when you want to lead people to the path of illumination: words and deeds.

Should you run away from evil forces and hand them the victory? Of course not. The best way to eradicate evil is to face it and fight it.

> **Key attitudes and behaviors to remember from Step 7:**
>
> - There are evil, anti-farting people out there, including people you thought love you. You should fight by farting freely
> - As a Free Farter, you are a superior human being

Actions and feelings log for Step 7:

	Freedom to fart	Feedback loop 1	Feedback loop 2	Feedback loop 3 etc.
Feel				
Act (underlined)				
Reflect				
Transcend				

SAMPLE – DO NOT WRITE HERE

Progress tracker for Step 7:

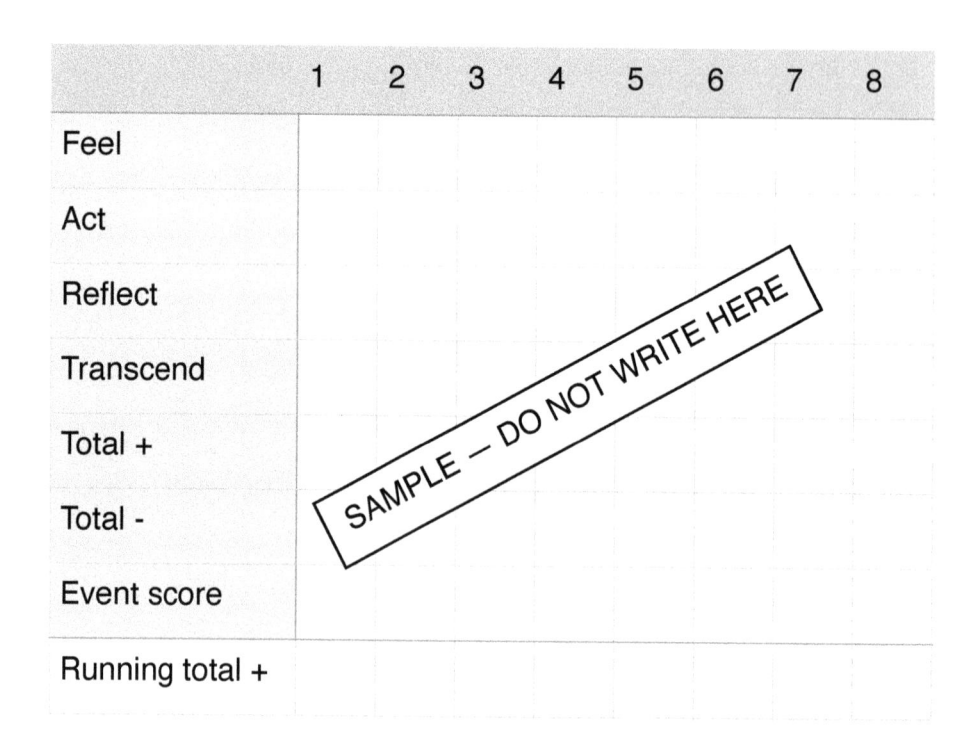

	1	2	3	4	5	6	7	8
Feel								
Act								
Reflect								
Transcend								
Total +								
Total -								
Event score								
Running total +								

SAMPLE – DO NOT WRITE HERE

11.
Conclusion

"One should never forbid what one lacks the power to prevent." —Napoleon Bonafarte

Unlike smoking, there isn't actually a law against farting, or self-imposed regulations akin to what you have in airplanes or inside airport terminals, many of which now have designated smoking areas. Nor is it like breastfeeding, which is frowned upon at restaurants. Feed the most vulnerable and dependent persons on Earth, and you risk being asked to leave a place where people are supposed to eat. What a hodgepodge of silly logic and irony!

Luckily, as Free Farters, we don't have to face any of these restrictions. Yet. The winds of liberty are not always blowing in our direction, as evidenced by two recent incidents that took place—not in far-flung dictatorships with questionable human rights practices—but in highly developed democracies with near-impeccable track records.

Sweden 2016: Expelled for Expelling—Sent off Football Field for Farting

A Swedish footballer had a bad stomach and had to fart during a match. That qualified for a second yellow card, which meant he was sent off—with the referee accusing him of "deliberate provocation" and "unsportsmanlike behavior". Excuse me? Aren't sportsmen and women supposed to take good care of their bodies? What better way than to listen to its signals and act without undue delay, like getting off the field for treatment when injured?

When asked whether you are not allowed to fart on a football field, the referee simply answered, "No." We have insufficient information to classify the referee according to our framework, but my gut feeling is that he is an ignorant wannabe dictator.

Netherlands/Austria 2018: Sent off Airplane for Sending Air Back Into the Air

An equally disturbing incident took place aboard an airplane bound for the capital of The Netherlands, in many ways the cradle of modern Western freedom. Apparently, two passengers thought they were getting an overdose of arthritis vaccines kindly provided by a Free Farter sitting next to them, farting loud and clear. Although the exact medical justification for capping the sulfur intake remains unclear, facts suggest that the passengers were anti-vaccinationists and believed their humans rights were being violated. In other words, there were basically two different human rights camps—Free Farters vs. anti-vaccinationists—at loggerheads over differences of opinion in a confined space.

The captain, who evidently qualifies as an ignorant wannabe dictator, made a so-called emergency landing in Austria, where, ironically, the police boarded the plane with dogs—creatures that always fart when needed.

What happens next is worthy of a dictatorship. Believe it or not, but the freely farting hero was escorted off the airplane, and so was his travel companion as well as two young women sitting next to them! On what grounds? Judging by the facts, for being accessories to farting. Has the world gone mad? Not only did they fail to recognize the Free Farter as a hero, but they actually sent him off the airplane, along with three fellow passengers who were lucky enough to sit next to him. Forget global warming—we may be able to blame it on volcanic activity with more data available. Forget wars—there have always been wars and always will be. The same goes for crazy dictators and tweetoholic presidents. All of this is just part of the world as we know it. But sending someone off an airplane for being an **accessory to farting**? The world *has* gone mad—no doubt about it. Unfortunately, the search for inhabitable exoplanets has barely made minor advances, so we are stuck on Earth for the time being.

Despite these attacks on our way of life, we live in hope:

- Hope that our way of life won't be banned

- Hope that we will be respected

- Hope that more people will go down our path

- Hope that the self-sacrifice we make by—in other people's view—embarrassing ourselves in public will lead to extended civil rights across the globe

- Hope that one day we will live in complete, unfettered freedom

Unleash your Inner Windhorse and Avoid Bad Karma

Much like the historically speaking pacific people of Tibet, who have faced formidable adversaries over the centuries and organized resistance movements contradictory to their fundamental beliefs, there comes a time when you need to rely on your own ability to face and fight evil. One of the resistance heroes of the novel "Windhorse" realized that it was futile to rely solely on the prayer flags or windhorses that scattered prayers across the lands and up to the heavens. He concluded: "We are the windhorse now", the horse that "is carrying us all to liberation". Are we too as aspiring or actual Free Farters facing a formidable enemy? You bet.

Not simply a prayer flag adorning buildings and hilltops across Central Asia, the windhorse is an important animal in Tibetan and Mongolian mythology and essentially an allegory for the human soul in their shamanistic tradition. Interestingly, its name in Mongolian translates literally to "gas horse". Coincidence? I think not. It has also been described as a subtle flow of energy called *rLung*, something like our "inner air" on which the mind rides. Like a horseman, the mind needs something strong to ride on in order to ride properly.

Does that mean that our souls are in our farts, or vice versa? I would argue yes.

> *Last night the Windhorse came to visit me*
> *I thought he wanted to take me riding*
> *Into cosmos beyond time and space,*
> *Instead he wanted to merge with me*

(Windhorse, Poems of Illumination by Ayn Cates Sullivan)

The above excerpt is from a poem which is probably about love-making, but it may just as well be about farting in the presence of your partner. We listen to our bodies when we feel an urge, and we are all short-lived amoebas on the face of the Earth, minuscule parts that make up an immense, ever-changing totality. This is referred to as *impermanence*, the fact that everything changes constantly. We constantly merge with other people's windhorses, as we breathe their farts or eat minute recycled particles from their decayed bodies.

We as Free Farters easily identify ourselves with the windhorse because it:

subdues evil
is fearless
is a vehicle of enlightenment
makes us think positively when it is strong
is a symbol of well-being or good fortune

The last characteristic has been my exact point all along—farting is good for your health and your career. Forget about the subtle frowning around the cubicles in your office or by the passengers sitting behind you in your Yellow Cab. These people simply don't know what's good for them. I say, go with the flow, the *rLung*.

Not only are representatives of the enemy—those who get cross when you fart—devoid of hope and understanding, they also harbor all Three Poisons in Tibetan Buddhism, depicted by a pig, a snake and a cockerel. The pig represents ignorance or delusion, the snake means anger or ill will, and the cockerel means desire or greed, in this case the desire for a fart-free world.

Undoubtedly, anti-farters can only dream of being reborn as anything with half a brain, if we are to believe the Buddhist creed and the idea of reincarnation.

Who Are You and Who Do You Want to Be, in This Life and the Next?

As we know, anti-farters come in different guises. I have demonstrated that people can be classified into one of the following five categories:

1) Free Farters (or enlightened promoters)
2) Evil bastards (or aware opponents—those who are against free farting, even if they are aware of the benefits) (Key Idea # 8)
3) Selfish argon holes (aware self-opponents—those who are aware of the benefits of farting but choose to fart alone)
4) Ignorant wannabe dictators (unaware opponents—those who don't know why free farting is good for you but still oppose it)
5) Useful idiots (unaware promoters—those who are unaware of the physiological and spiritual benefits of farting freely but still promote it)

There is no middle ground or room for pragmatism here. You can't say, "I'm a Free Farter at heart, but you have to assess the situation and the people around you there and then." Or: "I fart alone, not because I am selfish but because my farts smell really bad." If they smell bad, they are full of the good stuff, remember?

Now that you know how farting freely contributes to a Better You on so many fronts, and knowing that all people, including pop stars, ventriloquists, gas meter readers, and mass murderers, fall into one and only one of the above categories, look in the mirror and ask yourself, "Who am I? Who do I aspire to be?"

Since you made it to the end of this book without soiling your underwear and blaming me, the answer is given: **congratulations**—you are your own windhorse and a member of the exclusive club of Free Farters! The more members we have, the more likely it is that we will make the move from marginalized to mainstream.

The Trombones of Triumph are ready to roar and will soon fill the air around all of us!

When they do, we will all love our own farts because:

1) The day you stop farting permanently, you are dead

2) They get their energy from the Big Bang. How awesome is that?

3) They are like vitamins, and you don't need to remember to take them

4) You can issue an unlimited farting prescription to yourself and there is no way you can overdose

5) I ❤ MOF makes a great bumper sticker

6) They break awkward silence

7) You give pieces of yourself to the world

8) They enliven boring relationships

9) You have probably re-farted parts of dinosaur farts. That's just too cool!

10) They surprise you with unexpected smell or sound every time. Surprise is an important ingredient in healthy, long-lasting relationships

* * * A Very Happy End to All * * *

Appendix:
Process for Determining Social Acceptability of Biologically Driven Human Behavior

If you can answer YES to all these questions, then do it:

Is it human?

Is it natural?

Is it harmless?

Is it legal?

Is it transient i.e. generally unpleasant for less than one minute, if at all?

Will it go unpunished, meaning is the risk of being hanged, drawn and quartered negligible?

Take spitting. It's human and natural, for sure. You get a fly in your mouth, and you spit it out. It can, however, be harmful if you have some infectious disease. It can also be unpleasant for more than one minute if you spit on the floor in someone's bedroom. Clearly, spitting is out in many situations, especially indoors or around fellow citizens.

The same logic applies to sneezing, coughing and picking your nose. Vomiting is just spitting on steroids, so clearly out.

How about smoking? It's human; no need to debate that. Natural? Probably. Over thousands of years, humans have tried to consume all sorts of plants in all sorts of ways, either as food or for some sort of pleasure. Smoking is, however, considered harmful by most experts, as is passive smoking, which can also be unpleasant. Hence, you can't smoke everywhere or in every situation.

Having sex publicly is another activity many people disapprove of. It's human, by definition. Despite some artificial remedies and accessories being used in certain circles, it's quite natural. Most of the time, it's a pleasure, so generally harmless—until there's a traffic accident because car drivers watch the act rather than focusing on the road.

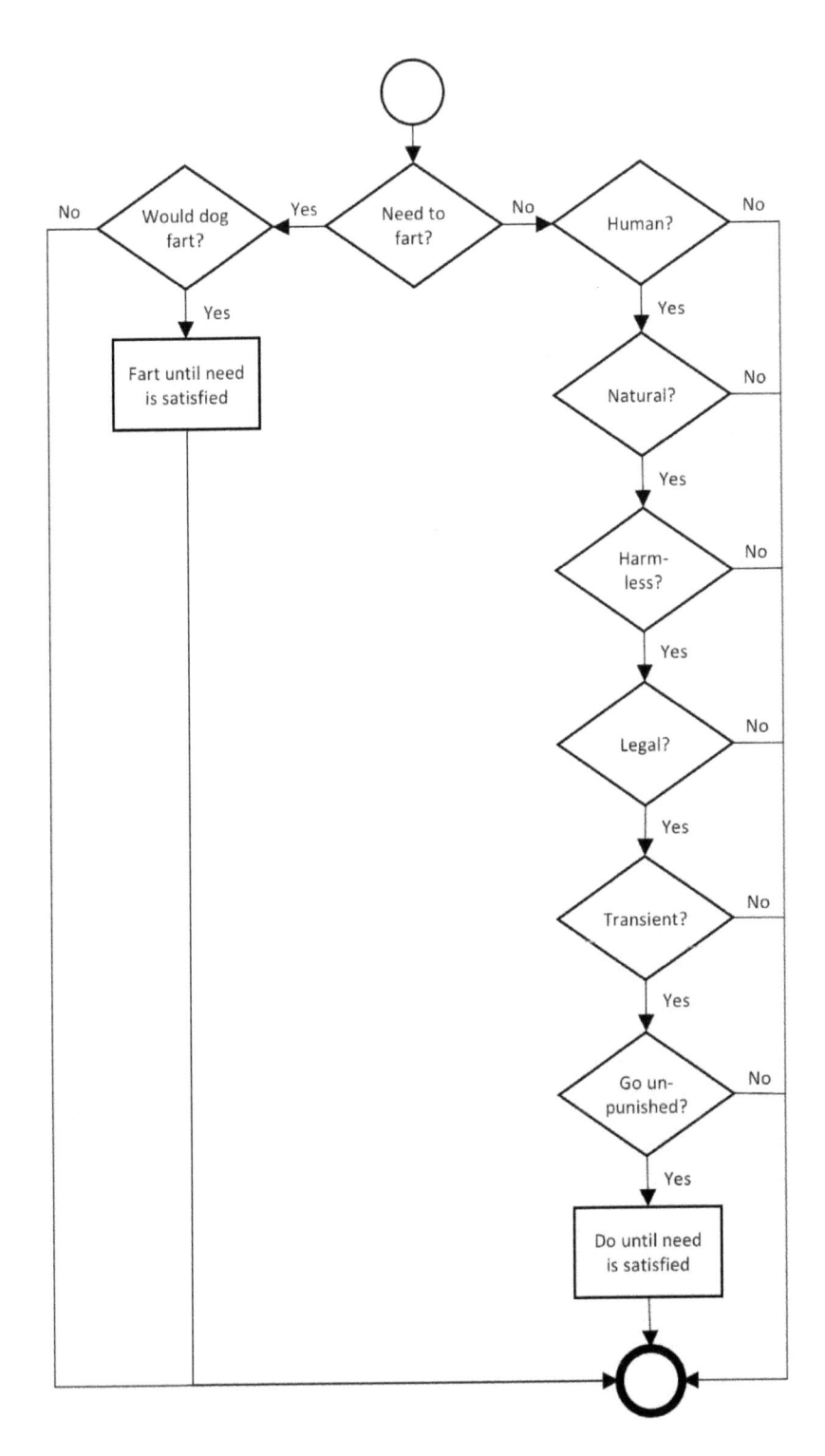

```
                          ┌─────────┐
                          │    ○    │
                          └────┬────┘
                               ▼
      No    ┌──────────┐ Yes ┌──────────┐ No  ┌──────────┐  No
    ◄───────│ Would dog │◄────│  Need to │─────│  Human?  │────────┐
            │   fart?   │     │   fart?  │     │          │        │
            └─────┬─────┘     └──────────┘     └────┬─────┘        │
                  │ Yes                              │ Yes          │
                  ▼                                  ▼              │
          ┌───────────────┐                   ┌──────────┐  No      │
          │ Fart until need│                  │ Natural? │──────────┤
          │  is satisfied │                   └────┬─────┘          │
          └───────┬───────┘                        │ Yes            │
                  │                                ▼                │
                  │                         ┌──────────┐  No        │
                  │                         │  Harm-   │────────────┤
                  │                         │  less?   │            │
                  │                         └────┬─────┘            │
                  │                              │ Yes              │
                  │                              ▼                  │
                  │                         ┌──────────┐  No        │
                  │                         │  Legal?  │────────────┤
                  │                         └────┬─────┘            │
                  │                              │ Yes              │
                  │                              ▼                  │
                  │                         ┌──────────┐  No        │
                  │                         │Transient?│────────────┤
                  │                         └────┬─────┘            │
                  │                              │ Yes              │
                  │                              ▼                  │
                  │                         ┌──────────┐  No        │
                  │                         │  Go un-  │────────────┤
                  │                         │punished? │            │
                  │                         └────┬─────┘            │
                  │                              │ Yes              │
                  │                              ▼                  │
                  │                      ┌───────────────┐          │
                  │                      │ Do until need │          │
                  │                      │  is satisfied │          │
                  │                      └───────┬───────┘          │
                  │                              ▼                  │
                  └─────────────────────────►( ● )◄─────────────────┘
```

Figure i

Acknowledgements

My anus—Its incessant cries for help while trapped in dirty underwear have made me aware of a critical bodily function and inspired me to write this book. The subliminal messages it sent to encourage me to write this book were not at all subliminal, as I am convinced I heard the word "book" many times.

The brewing industry—Thank you for countless memorable moments.

K. M. B. and G. K.—Two colleagues who read through an early manuscript and encouraged me to write the book. Their initials have been encrypted and re-encrypted backwards to protect their anonymity.

Frank Cantoneso—A colleague and lawyer who assessed the risk that I will be sued if someone is injured when farting close to open fire, and found it passable.

About the Author

CHRIS DAREWIND has been sitting on his rear end—and trying to find deeper meaning in the signals it sends—in a corporate office in Oslo for most of his adult life, which spans more than three decades. One day, he decided to use artificial intelligence to blend his infinite supply of one-liners with equally many embarrassing episodes featuring flatulence in a key role. The result is his first and probably only book. The only natural eruption he fears is the volcanic kind, having fled from one while stationed in Africa as an aid worker.